PAMELA MAASS GARRETT

ESTATE PLANNING FOR PARENTS

THE **6 STEP PLAN** TO
PROTECT YOUR CHILDREN'S
HAPPINESS AND FUTURE

Published by Best Seller Publishing®, St. Augustine, FL
Best Seller Publishing® is a registered trademark.
Printed in the United States of America.
ISBN: 978-1-956649-26-0

This publication is designed to provide accurate and authoritative information with regard to the subject matter covered. It is sold with the understanding that the publisher is not engaged in rendering legal, accounting, or other professional advice. If legal advice or other expert assistance is required, the services of a competent professional should be sought. The opinions expressed by the authors in this book are not endorsed by Best Seller Publishing® and are the sole responsibility of the author rendering the opinion.

For more information, please write:
Best Seller Publishing®
53 Marine Street
St. Augustine, FL 32084
or call 1 (626) 765-9750
Visit us online at: www.BestSellerPublishing.org

FOR MY HUSBAND AND MY DAUGHTER,

MY "HAPPILY EVER AFTER"!

Once upon a time, I decided to write a book. It was so much harder, yet so much more rewarding than I had expected.

First upon a time, I would like to thank my wonderful husband, my love and my best friend, Andrew Garrett. Your love and your support grant me the confidence and boldness to follow our dreams.

My love and appreciation for my parents are reflections of their love, believing in me and supporting me throughout life, and also through my efforts with this book. Thank you for spending your vacation brainstorming the title with me and for proofreading the drafts I sent your way. Thank you for encouraging me to persevere and, most of all, thank you for encouraging me to reach for the stars.

Thank you to my big brother, Dave, who helped me write my first article for the Bear Essential News. Your talent for writing is inspiring.

Sincerest gratitude to my mentor, Ali Katz, founder of New Law Business Model and creator of the Personal Family Lawyer brand and new way of being a lawyer. I am a Personal Family Lawyer as I write this acknowledgment, and I encourage readers to learn more at https://personalfamilylawyer.com. You have inspired me, guided me to build a business I truly love, and changed the course of my life. Your mentorship, leadership, and guidance made this book possible.

Thank you to Bonnie Faucett for your support, mentorship and friendship. The systems and processes you've developed have improved my business and life. You have made a huge impact in my life.

Thank you to my wonderful editor and book coach, Chrissy Das. Your encouragement, insights, and Saturday morning Zoom meetings brought this book to the finish line.

Thank you, Nicole Schryver, for helping me produce the first draft of this book, and for your friendship.

I really appreciate my lifelong friends, Shayna Labadie, Alison Edelstein, Holly Hart, Lisa Duran, Heidi Wilbur, Ashley Ahrens, Nikole Rachelson and Adrian Van Nice for your input on the book and for your love and support.

I am grateful to the Law Mother team: Aly Gardiner, Jorge Esparza, Naomi Arana, and Sara Walter. Life is a team sport; I am grateful to have you on my team.

Tom Bowles, thank you for going above and beyond to help us share our message digitally.

Thank you to the Best Seller Publishing team, who are helping me through the publishing process.

Thank you to my professional mentors: Jennifer Eyl, Tamara Kuennen, John Gleason, John Clune, Stan Garnett, Sean Finn, Michael Foote, Paul Johnson, Ross Pulkrabek, Robert Kraus, Steve Morgan, and Dan Williams.

Thank you to all the Personal Family Lawyers for your guidance, encouragement, and friendship.

Thank you to the coaches and teachers that have inspired, mentored, and transformed me: Lindsay Dotzlaf, Benita Samuels, Melanie Lippman, Allison Osborn, Ceri Payne, Krista Gano, Amy Scerra, Steve Haase, Josh Levin, Jessica Anguiano, Eric Farone, Erica Teel, Kristina Hall, Clare Ochoa, Eric Scheele, Ariel Krassner, Brooke Castillo, Anita Lee, and RJon Robins.

Thank you to the BNI Westside Empire. When I signed up for weekly 7:30am meetings, it was because I thought it could improve my business. I continue to show up each week because you've improved my life. You are an amazing community, and I am so grateful for you.

Appreciation to the Colorado Women Owned Law Firm group. You have helped me rise to the challenges.

Thank you to the Inner Circle Mastermind. Our monthly accountability and mastermind calls have kept me focused.

I appreciate my Firestorm group. You continue to challenge me and open my eyes.

Thank you to the Northwest Douglas County Chamber and the Next Level Networking Group. The camaraderie, support, and encouragement are greatly appreciated.

Thank you to the Mamistad Mom's Group. I survived and thrived during pregnancy, postpartum, and now with a toddler thanks to your friendship and our community.

Finally, thank you to my friends, family, and colleagues for all your support and love.

CONTENTS

INTRODUCTION

"A dream is a wish your heart makes when you're fast asleep."

—*Cinderella*

Growing up, my parents read me the story of Cinderella, an orphan mistreated by her evil stepmother and stepsisters. Cinderella's happily ever after starts with the help of her fairy godmother and ends with her in the arms of a prince.

Thinking about the story today as both a mom and a lawyer, I find myself considering an alternative option. A legally happily ever after, which starts with an estate plan and ends with Cinderella's protected inheritance and a loving caregiver. After all, Cinderella's parents would never have wanted their daughter to lose everything and become a servant in her own home.

WHAT IS ESTATE PLANNING, EXACTLY?

In simple terms, estate planning is the process of making sure that your wishes are carried out for you and your family if something happens to you.

With proper estate planning, a magical fairy godmother isn't necessary to implement a meaningful transfer of money to your loved ones and to be sure they are taken care of. In other words, if Cinderella's family had created an estate plan, she would have been able to process the grief of losing both parents and would not have had to also suffer the loss of her childhood home.

While the Cinderella story may have been fictional, there are many young and adult children all over the world who are being taken advantage of like Cinderella. These families did not properly plan their estate before they died and therefore caused their own children to be deprived of what is rightfully theirs in an inheritance.

For the sake of your children and their future, estate planning is a way to protect them from not only being taken advantage of but also to protect their future and happiness. The goal of this book is to provide you with a roadmap to protect your children's future and happiness through L.E.G.A.C.Y., a six-step plan:

L - Legal Guardians
E - Economic Support
G - Guidance
A - Asset Protection
C - Carry Through, Communicate & Update
Y - Your Family Legacy

Without a plan, your family is left with a mess—and, for many families, a nightmare!

Andrew's Nightmare

Andrew's grandfather never put an estate plan in place. Andrew remembers his father and uncle fighting about how long to keep his grandfather on life support. Andrew remembers his dad pacing around the living room as he made calls to organize his grandfather's affairs when he died. Andrew's father and uncle don't spend holidays together anymore; there's a wedge between them that has affected his entire family.

Andrew and his wife hired my law firm to put an estate plan in place because they don't want their sons to go through what his dad and uncle did. Andrew is also concerned about who would care for his 7- and 5-year-old if something happened to him and his wife, especially since he's not close to his cousins and other family members.

Our firm put together an estate plan that clearly names who will care for their kids if something happens while their children are minors. Andrew chose some close friends and put together a memorandum with instructions. Andrew and his wife secured their assets in a living trust to keep things organized for their children. Our firm also set up the right protections, so that his kids won't lose their inheritance through future divorces, creditors or bad decisions.

Estate planning doesn't have to be complicated, but it should be personalized for your family's specific needs. This book will help you understand what legal documents you need and why you need them, while preparing you to find the best possible attorney for your needs. With this book, you will learn how to lay out very specific ground rules for your assets, your estate and how your children will be cared for.

1

LEGALLY EVER AFTER DOESN'T HAPPEN BY DEFAULT

"Even miracles take a little time."

—*Cinderella*

My husband and I were sitting in the movie theater on a date night waiting for the show to start. He asked me what would happen to our daughter if we didn't make it home safely that night and we hadn't put an estate plan in place. We live in Colorado and all of our blood relatives live thousands of miles away, in Arizona, California and Iowa.

I told my husband if we didn't make it home and we didn't yet have an estate plan in place, our babysitter would call the police. The police would call child protective services. A stranger from child protective services would show up at the house and take our daughter from our home and bring her to a foster home. That would be very scary for our daughter, to have to leave her home and go live with someone she never met.

Then, our parents and siblings would have to travel to Colorado, find and hire lawyers and request they open a court case. This court case would be in front of a stranger, a judge who would decide who would care for our daughter. We hope our families will get along, but they may not agree on who should raise our kids. Additionally, the judge might not select the person we'd want to raise our child.

The situation I just described is scary and unsettling as a parent. Thankfully, we have an estate plan in place that we revisit every three years. Unfortunately, a family without an estate plan is not rare. As a former Deputy District Attorney, I saw this situation happen over and over again. Families did not have access to the legal planning tools I describe in this book; an accident would happen, and Child Protective Services or foster care would take their children until the courts could sort it out. I saw this problem, and I knew I wanted to help families plan ahead to avoid it.

It is scary to think about who would raise your kids if you could not. Often, the discomfort of thinking about it prevents people from putting a plan in place. However uncomfortable it is to think about it, the alternative, "do nothing" approach, is much worse. Having a plan in place gives you the peace of mind that no matter what, your family will be taken care of the way you'd want and that your choices would be honored. A plan ensures your children will never be with strangers, that they will be in the care of those you love and trust.

Unfortunately, the fear of putting a plan in place is not the only fear that keeps parents from planning. The following myths about estate planning are often a barrier to protecting your loved ones.

MYTHS ABOUT ESTATE PLANNING

Myth One: If I Prepare a Plan, Something Will Happen to Me

I totally understand this fear, and I hear this a lot from my clients—this idea that if I put an estate plan in place, then something will happen to me. I will die unexpectedly. The good news is: of the thousands of cases I've worked on, I've seen no type of correlation or connection between putting an estate plan in place, and then something happening accidentally or suddenly.

The reality is, at some point, we will all pass on. When the time comes, your loved ones will appreciate you taking the time now to put all your ducks in a row. Unfortunately, the alternative "do nothing" approach will often result in your family going through the probate process, which is time-consuming and costly.

Myth Two: I Am Too Young to Make a Plan

A question I get asked a lot—am I too young to put together an estate plan? The answer is no. There isn't a set age and there's a common myth that you have to be elderly to have an estate plan in place. Really, that doesn't serve people because a lot of times it's a type of planning that if you procrastinate putting in place and then something unexpected happens—it's too late. Additionally, when people wait until they are unhealthy to put a plan in place they often aren't making the best decisions.

Life Event Checklist: When Should You Update or Create Your Estate Plan?

The following checklist gives you some guidance on when you should create or update your estate plan based on life events.

Your Life Event Checklist

Have any of these events happened to you this year?

If you check one or more boxes below, it's time to update or create your estate plan.

- ☐ You reviewed your estate plan 5+ years ago
- ☐ Birth of first child, or children have turned 18 (or older)
- ☐ Got Married
- ☐ Got Divorced or remarried
- ☐ Individuals previously named are no longer appropriate

☐ Moved to a different state/relocated to or from a different state

☐ Have had a significant increase/decrease in the value of your assets

☐ Bought a vacation home or rental property

☐ Changed your primary residence

☐ You have an IRA, 401(k), or other qualified plan that requires you to begin to take distributions.

Myth Three: I Am Not Wealthy Enough to Make a Plan

Dave and Naomi

Dave and Naomi are a young married couple with two kids under the age of ten. They are an average middle-class couple; they own a home and they are saving up for their future. Dave's brother and dad are drug addicts. Dave and Naomi have sizeable life insurance plans and fear that if they were to die, Dave's brother and dad would try and get custody of their children. We put together a comprehensive estate plan to ensure that Dave and Naomi's assets and children are fully protected and kept out of the hands of their drug-addicted family members.

It's not about how much money you have, it's about how much input you want to have.

Without an estate plan, you are at the mercy of the government to make your decisions. Ultimately, a stranger, a judge will make the decision about who will care for you financially and medically if you become disabled. Unfortunately, most of us will become disabled at some time in our life. Additionally, a judge will decide who will care for your kids if they are minors, and if your children are adults they will receive their inheritance outright with no asset protection and without guidance.

Many people think they don't have enough money to pay for an estate plan. However, the cost of no plan is much more than the cost of a plan. The default plan if you do not have an estate plan is probate court. This is costly and inconvenient; on average it costs 5-9% of your estate and takes between 9 months and two years. For example, a family with a $400k home, $500,000 in life insurance and $100,000 in retirement accounts will lose $50,000-$90,000 in probate. Alternatively, by creating an estate plan with a qualified attorney, they will avoid the $50,000-$90,000 in probate costs and only pay the estate plan costs between $4,000-$6,000.

Myth Four: All I Need is a Simple Will

Many parents believe all they need is a simple will to protect their loved ones. Unfortunately, a will alone is not enough. A will doesn't cover what happens if you're incapacitated or disabled. A will also has to go through the probate court, be filed with the court, and a court case is actually commenced in order for a will to be effective.

What is probate?

Probate is a court process. Each state has their own probate court process. During the probate process, a judge decides how assets are transferred. It is a court proceeding.

When your family members or loved ones have to go through probate to help you or your estate, they get a case number. There are court fees, legal fees and you are reliant on the timetable of the courts. On average, the probate process takes 9 months to two years and costs 5-9% of your estate value.

The probate process also gets involved if there is a minor child or incapacitated adults. The judge will decide who will be in charge of the financial affairs and the medical decisions for the minor or incapacitated adult.

The probate court gets involved when you pass away or become incapacitated and have a will in place, or if you have no plan in place. However, you can create an estate plan that avoids probate.

If you haven't created an estate plan that will avoid probate, you're leaving it up to a probate judge to figure out who's in charge of your finances if you're incapacitated, and who becomes guardian of your children if something happens to you.

Myth Five: If I am Married My Spouse Will Automatically Be in Charge

If you are married, you still need a plan. Without one, your spouse will likely have to deal with frozen bank accounts when you pass away. They will have to go to court to be able to make decisions if you become disabled. Without a plan, your spouse will lose out on the opportunity to minimize the taxes paid and will not have the benefits of asset protection. Additionally, eventually both of you will die and some action will need to be taken with your remaining assets.

There is a common misconception that if you are ever incapacitated or disabled, your spouse will automatically be able to act on your behalf. However, this is not true.

The law does not assume that your spouse has your best interest. Therefore, absent a legal plan in place, your spouse would have to go to probate court to ask the judge to make your medical and financial decisions. If a family member wishes to make your medical or financial decisions, for example your parents or a sibling, they can ask the judge to appoint them as financial or medical guardians. One of the most famous examples of this is the Terri Schiavo case.

In the early morning of February 25, 1990, Terri Schiavo collapsed in the hallway of her St. Petersburg, Florida apartment. The cause of Terri's collapse was determined to be cardiac arrest. Losing oxygen to her brain during the time prior to being resuscitated caused damage to her brain. After two and a half months without improvement, her doctors changed her diagnosis to that of a persistent vegetative state. At this point, Terri was being kept alive by artificial means.

Initially, the court appointed her husband Michael as her legal guardian. In 1998, he filed a petition with the court asking to disconnect Terri's feeding tube. Terri's parents opposed the removal of her feeding tube. Because Terri had never formally expressed her wishes regarding end-of-life treatment, nor had she appointed an Agent to make decisions for her, an epic legal battle began that ripped her family apart. It tore apart not just a family, but the nation, too, as many people chose sides. The saddest part of all is it could have all been avoided if Terri Schiavo simply had executed an advance health directive prior to her collapse.

**Check out your free companion
course for added support and bonuses:**
LegallyEverAfter.com/Resources

2

L - LEGAL GUARDIANS: NAME GUARDIANS FOR YOUR CHILDREN

"A dream is a wish your heart makes."

—Brothers Grimm, 'Cinderella'

If Cinderella's father had a do-over, he would have picked a more suitable guardian for Cinderella.

Selecting and planning for guardians of your children in the event of your death is not easy to think about. However, the alternative, do nothing approach is much worse. If you don't choose guardians, it will be up to a judge to make that decision for you.

The history of guardianship extends back to the Roman Empire, when it was understood that parents and extended family were legally responsible for supporting children. In feudal times, they deemed the father the legal guardian for children. Upon the death of the father, either the mother or the feudal lord would receive guardianship.

Today, guardians are typically named in four situations: guardian for a minor, guardian for a developmentally disabled adult, guardian for an incapacitated senior and guardian for an incompetent adult.

In 2019, 672,000 children were in the US foster care system. In 2020, the journal Pediatrics estimated 140,000 children in the US lost a parent or grandparent caregiver to COVID-19. "This means that for every four COVID-19 deaths, one child was left behind without a mother, father and/or a grandparent who provided for that child's home needs and nurture—needs such as love, security and daily care," says Susan Hillis, an epidemiologist at the Centers for Disease Control and Prevention and lead author of the new study.

A guardian for a minor is the person asked to take over and raise your child or children if you cannot.

This could be a friend, grandparent, relative, or anyone that you choose. The exact requirements a legal guardian must meet varies based on state law. Generally, guardians can be anyone over the age of 18 and who is of sound mind. The guardian will care for and raise your child. This could be the same person who controls the money for your child, or it could be a separate person.

IF I DIE WITHOUT A PLAN, WHO WILL TAKE CARE OF MY KIDS?

Naming a guardian for your children in the event both you and your children's other parent pass away or become incapacitated is one of the most difficult decisions a parent must make, but it's also one of the most important decisions. While the decision might be difficult, if you don't appoint a guardian, it will be up to a judge, a stranger, to make that decision for you. The dangers of having the court make these decisions are the timeframe, cost, and ultimately losing the ability to choose who ends up caring for your children.

Your relatives would have to open a court case to ask for guardianship of your child, and this process can take many months or even years. During that time, they may place your child in child protective services or foster care.

If there is conflict and no written plan, and people in your family disagree on whether that blood relative should take care of your kids, then your children may end up in child protective services until the court system can figure out who should raise your kids. The cost of these proceedings will be taken out of your child's inheritance and can often be thousands or tens of thousands of dollars.

The judge is going to decide who has the best interests of the child, and that might not be the same decision that you would make. For example, the judge might choose someone who looks really good on paper. However, that person might be someone you would actively avoid having around your children.

Nominating legal guardians as part of your estate plan fully protects your kids and ensures that your children would be raised by who you want, the way you want.

The Importance of Naming Short-Term Guardians

Cycling Emergency

Nicole Reynolds is a widow and has two children. Nicole decides to head out of state for a cycling and camping adventure with a group of families and her two kids. One morning, Nicole wakes up very early and goes for a ride with some friends and leaves her young kids at basecamp with their friend Sarah. Unfortunately, Nicole is hit by a car, badly injured and is transferred to a hospital unconscious. Meanwhile at basecamp, the kids are with Sarah.

If Nicole could communicate, she would tell the first responders that she trusts her friend Sarah and would like Sarah to care for her kids. However, Nicole cannot speak, and is unconscious. Unfortunately, in this situation, only a blood relative can take temporary guardianship of the kids. Since Sarah is not a blood relative, she cannot take care of the kids. The closest blood relative is several thousands of miles away in Northern Colorado. Child protective services take the children into care in Utah until the Colorado family can travel to Utah.

> *If Nicole would have named Sarah as a short-term or temporary guardian, Sarah would have been able to care for the children until the long-term guardians were available.*

For our clients, we name both short-term and long-term guardians. Short-term guardians receive the paperwork so that, if there was an emergency, they are ready to care for your kids. We also print wallet ID cards for our clients to carry with the names and phone numbers of their short-term guardians. That way, if there was ever an emergency, the first responders would check their wallet and call the people listed on the card. We also recommend that parents give the short-term guardianship info to their babysitters, nannies and friends when they travel.

What if I have relatives who I never want to raise my kids?

Lacey and Steven

Lacey and Steven are high school sweethearts and the parents of two energetic boys. They both work in the financial industry and they are very conservative with their investments and spending. Steven's mother and brother are alcoholics, and he hasn't talked to them in many years. Steven and Lacey worry if they were to die when the kids are still young, Steven's mother and brother would try to get control of their estate and put their kids at risk. Lacey and Steven meet with me, and we put together a plan to exclude Steven's mother and brother from their estate and exclude them as guardians.

If you have relatives who you would never want to raise your kids, you can absolutely designate that in your estate plan. I often ask my clients about the dynamics involved with their family and with the specific person they have in mind to raise their kids.

For example, you can include a confidential exclusion in your estate plan, naming the person you would never want to raise your kids. This information is kept confidential, unless the person someday asks to raise your kids.

Does the same person who manages the money also take care of my kids?

Three Sisters

Molly has two very different sisters: Cindy the accountant and responsible sister and Heather, the artist and free spirit. During my meeting with Molly, she realized that without a plan, a judge would likely name Cindy as the guardian of her children and trustee of the estate. However, she would never want Cindy to be the guardian of her children. Cindy's parenting style isn't aligned with Molly's and her kids have a stronger connection with Heather. Molly worries, though, that Heather is bad with money. I proposed a solution that is the best of both worlds—Heather can be the legal guardian for the kids and Cindy will be the trustee and manage the financial affairs. Molly is very happy with the proposal and feels grateful that her kids will have the support of both her sisters, and in a way that is also aligned with Molly's values.

It's completely up to you whether the person who manages the money is also the guardian. You can designate the same person to manage the money for your kids or you can name a separate person to manage the money for your kids.

For example, you may have a family member that you feel would take really good care of your kids, but you know they aren't the best with money. In that case, you would name someone separate in your estate plan to care for the children and the money.

My partner and I are having trouble selecting guardians, any advice?

I recommend the following five easy steps to naming legal guardians to protect your children:

- Step One: Each partner brainstorms a list of potential guardian names separately.

You and your partner should each brainstorm a list of five to ten people that you would want to raise your kids if you could not. The goal here is to not share your list yet with your partner, do this exercise separately. The key to a good brainstorm session is for there to be no judgment. This is the step that most people do wrong; they share the list too soon and cannot agree. Do not share your list with your partner just yet.

- Step Two: Create a list of your values.

Create a short list of three to five of your top values. This is criteria for evaluating the people you've brainstormed. For example, these criteria could include the current relationship these people have with your child, their parenting style and what location they live in.

- Step Three: Rank each person or couple based on the criteria.

Now rank each person based on each criteria. You can use a ranking of one to ten for this exercise, see example in the table below.

Criteria	Relationship with Kids	Similar Parenting Style	Location	Total
Steve & Mary	10	4	6	20
Greg & Danielle	7	7	2	16
Sara	5	3	3	11
Nicole & Patrick	9	1	4	14

Keep in mind, you can also designate whether you'd like the couple to serve only if they are still together, or that you would allow a certain person to serve as a guardian alone if there was eventually a death or divorce.

- Step Four: Combine your lists with your partner's list and select the top three together.

Now that each of you has your ranking, sit down as a couple and together select the top three from both lists. The order of the top three is a common challenge I've seen my clients struggle with. For example, maybe the wife wants her sister to be number one and the husband wants her brother to be number one. Try not to get caught up with the order at this stage. Ultimately, if something were to happen to you, the top person you selected may not be available and then it would go to the next person. Try to resolve conflict at this stage by agreeing who to keep on the list and who to eliminate.

I also recommend reaching out to the potential people on the list and discussing if they would be willing to fill this role. Normally, these conversations go extremely well and give you a lot of peace of mind around your decision.

- Step Five: Finalize the guardian nominations in a legal document.

The final step is to formally name the guardian nominations in a legal document. I have a free tool on my website for doing just that. Please visit LegallyEverAfter.com/Resources to access this document.

I am divorced, do my ex-wife and I need to agree on guardians?

Ex-Wife and New Boyfriend

Tim is divorced. Claire, his ex-wife, is engaged to a man who is abusive to Claire. Tim is working with his divorce attorney to see what restrictions and protections he could put in place for the shared parenting of their three children. Tim called our office, worried about if he was to die, what protections he could put in place to protect his kids from their soon-to-be step-father.

How a court would view guardianship documents in the case of a blended family will depend on the law in the state you live in and the current custodial relationship. It is important to speak with a qualified attorney to form a plan that complies with state law.

Generally speaking, if you have a good relationship with the other biological parent, it is preferred that the two of you work together to select guardians you both agree on in case both of you pass.

If you don't have a good relationship with the other biological parent, you can prepare guardianship documents stating your preferences, but ultimately if both of you were to pass a judge is going to evaluate things at that time and may or may not follow your choices.

In the case of Tim, the strategy he takes is going to depend on the state he is in and the family law cases. It is important for Tim to work with both his family law attorney and estate planning attorney to put a plan in place to protect his kids.

One strategy Tim could evaluate is preparing a memorandum with the information in support of the reason he would never want the step-father to be guardians of his children if he were to die. He should share this documentation with the trustees he's named so that they can step in and argue his wishes if Tim were to die.

**Check out your free companion
course for added support and bonuses:**
LegallyEverAfter.com/Resources

3

E – ECONOMIC SUPPORT: PROVIDE FOR YOUR FAMILY'S LONG-TERM NEEDS

"No matter how your heart is grieving, if you keep on believing, the dream that you wish will come true."

—Cinderella

What happens to my assets if something happens to me?

If you pass away with no type of estate plan, and you have no will or trust in place, then the state that you live in will fill in those gaps. It's going to be state law and the state law's plan for you. In most states, if you're married, then the majority of assets are going to go to your spouse. If you are not married, then the majority of assets are going to go to your children. However, if your children are under the age of 18, they will not be able to inherit directly and the court will have to appoint someone to manage the money for them.

Another issue that often arises if you pass away without a plan is that those assets are not available readily to your family. As previously discussed, your family will have to go through probate court, which costs them time and money: costing about

5% to 9% of the estate's financial value and taking between nine months and two years.

PROVIDING ECONOMIC SUPPORT FOR YOUR FAMILY: THE BENEFITS OF A LIVING TRUST

A living trust is a legal document, or trust, created during an individual's lifetime, where a designated person, the trustee, is given responsibility for managing that individual's assets for the benefit of the eventual beneficiary.

If Cinderella's father had created a living trust and appointed a trustee for his money, Cinderella would have received money for health, education, maintenance and support, and she wouldn't have been forced to dress in rags. When she grew old enough, Cinderella's dad's trust could have specified that Cinderella receive money to be able to buy her own home, and she could have led a nice life with her Prince Charming.

What is the difference between a will and a trust?

	Living Trust	Will
Avoids Probate Costs	☑ Yes	No
Provide for your care during a disability	☑ Yes	No
Quickly Settled	☑ Yes	No
Leave property to minor children	☑ Yes	No
Keep privacy after death	☑ Yes	No
Protection from court challenges	☑ Yes	No
Asset Protection	☑ Yes	No
Minimize Estate Taxes	☑ Yes	No

A will is a legal document that expresses the last wishes of a person. It only comes into effect at the death of the creator ("testator"). A major issue is that a will undergoes probate after the death of the creator. As previously discussed, probate is the court proceeding your loved ones would have to endure if you die either without a plan or with a will alone. Probate is both costly (5-9% of your estate) and time consuming (a court process that can take, on average, between nine months and two years). During that time, your family would not have access to your assets. A will-based plan also means your asset transfer will be public, because it is a public court process.

A living trust is also a legal document that transfers assets; it comes into effect during the creator's life. One of the primary advantages of a living trust is that there is no probate court, i.e., there is no court process. Avoiding the probate process saves time and money. A living trust also allows you to transfer your assets privately. Living trusts also give you the options to plan in a way to legally reduce estate taxes and protect family assets from future creditors and future divorces.

Additionally, living trusts allow for you to plan for your incapacity. If you were ever incapacitated and only had a will in place or nothing in place, your loved ones would have to go to court to get access to the money to take care of you, your family and your affairs. However, with a living trust, the court process is avoided, and you state exactly who you would want to manage your affairs if you were incapacitated.

Who should create a will-based plan?

In trust-based planning, a pour over will is usually created. In other words, people who have living trusts also have a will. A pour over will is created with the hopes it will never be used. A pour over will is a safety measure or stop gap. If the trust is properly funded, meaning the title and beneficiary designation for all of your assets are properly transferred to your trust, then a pour over will won't ever be used. However, if at the time of your passing there is an asset that is outside your trust, the pour over will direct the court to transfer the asset to the trust.

Some people choose to do a will-based plan, and never form a trust. For example, in some states, if you have under a certain amount of assets (i.e. $75,000) the probate process is expedited and less costly. If you aren't sure whether you want or need a will versus a trust, contact a lawyer who practices in your state and understands what would happen to your family in both scenarios. Most lawyers have a free initial consultation and will spend the time educating you based on your specific needs.

What information about my assets should I have available for my family if I die?

If the unexpected were to happen to you (or your parents, siblings, or grandparents) do your loved ones know where all of your assets are located? Do they know about that old retirement account even though you've lost the paperwork? Do you know how to find what your parents have? Is everything documented clearly in one place, easy to find? Or would your hard-earned resources become part of the $58B lost to the state government because your family doesn't know?

Now is the time to make sure you've documented what you have, that your parents have documented what they have, and the people that matter know where it all is and how to find and access everything you have and would leave behind.

If you don't create an inventory of what you have, then there's a good chance the assets you worked so hard to earn will be lost at your death.

Every state has a Department of Unclaimed Property. Your assets go to the state if they are not claimed by your relatives. In Colorado, the Department of Unclaimed Property has $512 Million dollars. In New York, the Department of Unclaimed Property has $16.5 Billion dollars.

A friend of mine told me that her father was at the hospital about to undergo emergency heart surgery and had not put together an estate plan. The nurses were wheeling him to the operating room and he was telling his daughter to write on her napkin the location of oil leases he had. She only wrote down a few before he was taken away. Luckily, he came out of that surgery and was just fine; if he hadn't survived, his daughter may not have been able to locate all of his assets. She would have had to take the role of an investigator, searching to find all of his assets. Many of us assume that when we die our loved ones will be notified of all of the assets we have. The reality is that doesn't happen. If you have not left behind documentation of what assets you have specifically, your loved ones risk never finding those assets.

Bottom line, make sure you have a detailed list of everything you own, including account numbers in a file. Let your loved ones know where this file is if you ever become incapacitated or pass away.

What happens to my real estate if I die?

What happens to your real estate when you pass away really depends on how it's titled. In Colorado, and in most states, if you own title to your house in joint tenancy with right of survivorship, then your real estate will automatically transfer to your spouse regardless of what your will says. If you own a piece of property with your ex-spouse and you forget to update it, and you think your will is going to cover it, it won't. The real estate will still transfer to that ex-spouse.

If you own property as tenants in common with other family members, if something were to happen to you, it's going to transfer to the family members. If you own property in your own name, then when you pass away, it's going to go through the probate court process.

If you own property in a trust, then the property will transfer to whomever you've indicated in your trust.

If you own property in a limited liability entity (i.e. a Limited Liability Company), then your property will transfer based on the corporate agreements. If the transfer of property isn't specified in the corporate agreements, then the property will go through probate.

The only way to transfer real property to a minor directly, and avoid probate, is through a trust.

What happens to my bank accounts if I die or become incapacitated?

If you have bank accounts solely in your name, regardless if you are married, these accounts will go through probate.

Married couples often think that if their spouse was ever incapacitated or passed away, they could automatically get access to the spouse's accounts. However, this is not true. Unless you are on your spouse's accounts you will not get access and you will have to go to court to get access.

Unfortunately, there is no default rule that you as the spouse should get financial access to the account if your loved one is incapacitated. Therefore, a family member of your spouse could challenge you being appointed and instead ask that they should be appointed.

A typical example would be wife is incapacitated in the hospital after a ski accident and husband needs to get access to her bank account to pay her medical bills. When the couple got married, they had separate accounts and never got around to adding each other to the account. The wife's sister comes to the hospital and believes she should be in charge of her sister's financial affairs. After all, a lot of the money in the accounts is from their family business. Unfortunately, in this situation, both the husband and sister would have to go to court and the judge would decide who should manage the bank accounts for the incapacitated wife.

What happens to my business if I die or become incapacitated?

If you own a business, it is important that you have a business succession plan in place so that your business doesn't go through probate. If you have nothing in place your business likely will go through the probate process, and a judge, a stranger, is going to decide about who's going to run the business and what's going to happen to it.

There are a lot of options for including your business as part of your estate plan. If it's a family business and you want a specific family member to take over, you can set up the right structures and procedures to make that happen. For example, if you want certain assets to be sold, certain assets to be kept, you can also indicate that.

What happens to my life insurance when I die?

If you pass away with life insurance, likely you have designated a beneficiary. The beneficiary designation will trump what you put in a will, similar to the real estate title. If you name minor children in your life insurance beneficiary designations, the minor children cannot inherit money directly. The life insurance proceeds will go through the probate court and a judge is going to decide about who's going to manage your money until your children reach the age of 18.

If you have a trust, your life insurance proceeds will avoid probate and will pass to your children in the manner you choose in your estate plan. For example, if you have minor children, you will designate in your trust exactly who you want to manage the money for your children until they reach the age you feel they are financially responsible enough to manage the money themselves.

One of the biggest mistakes I come across is when people go through a divorce and forget to update their beneficiary designations. Therefore, they leave their ex-spouse as the beneficiary on their life insurance policy. If they do this, and pass away, their ex-spouse inherits directly from their life insurance, regardless of what their will says.

How much economic support should I leave for my family?

If you are purchasing life insurance to provide economic support for your family, a good rule of thumb is to have enough coverage to replace your income and cover expenses for your dependents after you're gone. A good ballpark figure is 10 to 15 times your annual salary.

If you have a special needs child or adult, you should set up a special needs trust to be sure any inheritance is not going to prevent your child from being eligible to receive government benefits in the future.

What happens to my retirement accounts?

Retirement accounts operate the same way as life insurance accounts. If you have a beneficiary designee, you really want to make sure that that person is the right person. You really want to make sure that if it's going to a minor child, you're prepared to go through probate. Otherwise, you really want to put it into a trust, so that you, not a judge, decides who will manage the money for your children.

Put a plan in place to make it as easy as possible for your loved ones after you pass away.

**Check out your free companion
course for added support and bonuses:**
LegallyEverAfter.com/Resources

4

G – GUIDANCE: EXPRESSING WISHES FOR YOUR CARE OF LIFE AND CARE OF MINOR CHILDREN

"Have courage and be kind."

—Cinderella

Terri Schiavo was a 26-year-old happily married book-keeper in Florida. In 1990, Terri Schiavo suffered from a cardiac arrest; the lack of oxygen to her brain caused massive brain damage which left her in a persistent vegetative state.[1]

Despite undergoing extensive therapy and testing, her condition did not improve. She could not communicate for herself, and her treating physicians reported there was no chance of improvement. After eight years with no improvement, Terri's husband believed Terri would not want to continue with life support. Terri's parents disagreed and felt Terri should be kept alive. For 15 years, Terri remained on life support, unable to speak for herself as her loved ones battled it out in court. The litigation became nasty, public, and political.

---

[1]   https://www.mayoclinicproceedings.org/article/S0025-6196(11)61439-0/fulltext

If Terri had received the legal planning tools discussed in this chapter, her choices would have been known and honored. Additionally, 15 years of litigation expenses would have been avoided.

The guidance you pass on in your estate plan should include guidance for care for you if you become incapacitated or disabled, as well as for how your kids should be cared for if you are unable to fulfill your parental role due to death or disability.

What happens if I become incapacitated without a written plan?

If you're incapacitated or disabled and not able to speak for yourself or make and communicate your decisions, then your relatives and spouse will have to go to court and ask the judge for permission to make medical and financial decisions on your behalf. If there is a conflict, for example, your spouse wants to remove you from life support and your parents do not, then this conflict will be resolved by a judge.

A common misconception is that if you are incapacitated or disabled and you are married, then your spouse can automatically and exclusively act for you. Even though you're married, there is no presumption that your spouse has your best interest at heart. They would be required to go to the probate court before making any decisions without a Power of Attorney or similar documentation on file, just like anyone else would need to if they intended to act on your behalf. Don't rely merely on the fact that you're married to assume that your spouse gets to do that automatically for you and don't rely just on a will to cover all of your estate planning concerns.

GUIDANCE FOR MEDICAL DECISIONS

Guidance for Medical Decisions - Living Will

A Living Will (also known as an advanced health care directive in some states) sometimes is mistaken for a Last Will. A Living Will applies while you're still alive and gives guidance on your healthcare preferences. A Last Will gives guidance on your possessions and body after your passing. A Living Will clarifies at what time, after what number of days, would you want to be taken off life support. For example, you could specify you want to be on life support for seven days or seven years. It's completely up to you. The important thing is that you've thought about it ahead of time and put it in writing so that if your family finds you in the situation, they know what your choices are and can honor those choices.

Having a living will honors your choices, and also avoids conflict between family members.

Guidance for Medical Decisions - Medical Power of Attorney

A Medical Power of Attorney is a legal document used to appoint people to make medical decisions on your behalf if you cannot. A Medical Power of Attorney is also known as a Health Care Power of Attorney, Health Care Proxy, Durable Power of Attorney for Health Care and Power of Attorney Medical. Your medical power of attorney will follow your Living Will; however, if there is a gray area, that appointed person will be tasked with making the final decision. Designating a medical power of attorney avoids conflict down the road. Instead of a judge deciding, your medical power of attorney will decide.

Without a plan in place, family members often disagree about these tough decisions. These disagreements end up causing a lot of suffering for families and ultimately can end up in expensive and lengthy court battles. However, much of the cost and conflict can be avoided with a plan in place.

Guidance for How Kids Should Be Raised

When Sarah and Mark's first child was born, they drafted wills. Five years and one more kid later, those drafts remained unsigned. The holdup was they couldn't agree on the legal guardians. Sarah wanted her brother; Mark wanted his sister.

The discussions grew heated, and ultimately, they avoided the topic altogether.

Sarah owned a successful veterinary practice. We designed a business succession plan for what would happen to her veterinary practice when she dies or becomes incapacitated. This plan included specific instructions on who would take over and how they would take over. Sarah could pull from her existing employee handbooks and business plan to feel confident her business would be in good hands.

As a business owner, Sarah would never hand her business over to be managed by someone without giving that person any guidance or instructions. As a mom, she wanted to do the same thing for her kids. However, when it came to planning how her kids would be taken care of, she felt overwhelmed and unprepared. What Sarah felt is expected; as parents, we don't typically create a family handbook.

In Chapter 2, we discussed techniques for resolving this type of conflict and how to choose legal guardians. However, naming legal guardians is just the beginning. How do you want your kids raised? What educational, financial, and spiritual values are essential to you? You should include these answers in all of your planning documents and can help make up your family handbook.

Creating a plan doesn't have to be complicated. You have specific things, besides money, that you want to pass on to your children upon your death. Your estate plan should include details about your educational values, religious or spiritual values, and other values you would want to be sure to pass on.

You have a few options when creating a plan for the caregivers of your children. This plan can be in the form of a written memorandum, recordings, or conversations. Any way you choose to go, I recommend that parents of minor children and adult children with disabilities speak with the people they have named as guardians about their values and wishes. Many times parents tell me that these conversations turn out wonderfully, that the guardians feel very honored to have the role and get more involved with the children. These early conversations will make future transitions easier if the need arises.

CREATE AN INSTRUCTIONS TO GUARDIANS MEMORANDUM

An Instructions to Guardians Memorandum provides guidance to the guardians of your minor children if you are unable to care for your children due to death or disability. The memorandum gives guidance with respect to those decisions you consider most important when raising our children, including education, religion and discipline, children-rearing practices, financial considerations, and your wishes regarding your children's care.

The memorandum can be in written form, or you can record your answers to the following questions. Whichever form you decide to create, the important thing is that you communicate your wishes to the guardians before something happens to you or inform them of where they can find this documentation if something were to happen to you.

The following items can be included in this memorandum:

1. **List of Important Family Members and Friends.** This list provides the names of friends and family members that are extremely important to you and your request that every effort should be made for these people to maintain a relationship with your children.
2. **Medical Information.** You should list out the current treatment providers for your children, any allergies, conditions, treatments and prescriptions.
3. **Activities and Extracurriculars.** You should list out which extracurricular programs and activities are important to your children.
   a. Include lessons and clubs that they are interested in, or plan to join at a later date.

b. Also include any activities that you have decided as a family that they *shouldn't* do.

4. **Financial.** While you have structured in your estate plan to provide for your children financially through your living trust, you may have additional financial guidance include the following:

a. We consider the following priorities the most important when it comes to the use of the financial resources we have left for our children:

b. We would like our children to receive an allowance at the following ages and in the following amounts:

c. We would like our guardian to teach our children the value of money in the following ways:

d. The following is a list of items we would expect our children to ask us for money and which we would help him with, if asked:

5. **Community**

a. We would like our children to be introduced to the following organizations and activities that support the community:

b. We have the following charitable inclinations and would like these to be further developed in our children:

6. **Values**

a. The personal values that are most important to us and that we would like our children to have a strong understanding of are as follows:

7. **Religion and Spirituality**

a. Our children have been raised in the following religion or tradition:

b. It is important to us that our children observe the following holidays:

c. It is important to us that our children participate in the following religious community:

8. **Education**
   a. We strongly prefer that our children attend public, private, home, other type of schooling:
   b. In selecting and monitoring our children's educational experiences, it is important to us that the guardian be closely involved in our children's education by:
   c. In addition, it is important that our guardian round out our children's education by providing opportunities outside of the classroom to enjoy:

9. **Discipline**
   a. The following methods of discipline are totally unacceptable to us, and if our guardian feels he or she requires these methods, we wish that person to decline to accept guardianship of our children:
   b. The following methods of discipline are those we use most frequently because we believe they are appropriate and effective:

10. **Parenting Resources**
   a. The following resources (books, organizations, etc.) have been helpful to us as we have developed our parenting philosophy. We encourage our children's guardian to consider these resources for himself or herself:

You can view an example Instructions to Guardian Memorandum on LegallyEverAfter.com/resources.

Greg and Alyson's Instructions to Guardian Memorandum

Greg and Alyson are successful young entrepreneurs. At age 30, they own several thriving companies and multiple investment properties. They have created a lifestyle where they spend quality time with their three children. Alyson's father, an entrepreneur himself, runs three successful restaurants. However, Alyson's father is still an employee. He works long hours and never has time for the family or vacation. While Alyson loves and respects her father, she is concerned about naming him as a potential financial guardian for her children if something happens to Greg and her. He doesn't share the values they are raising their children to have. Alyson and Greg brainstormed names of alternative financial guardians for their children and quickly became frustrated. For example, their friend Mark invests in cryptocurrency; they would never want him investing their money in cryptocurrency.

Greg and Alyson's reaction was expected; it is challenging to brainstorm someone who could replace you. However, the guidance memorandum is a powerful tool to bridge this gap. I redirected Greg and Alyson to the facts; their estate and life insurance will leave over $7 million to their kids if something happens when they are young. These children will be well taken care of. The key to naming a financial guardian is choosing people you trust to be good stewards and follow your memorandum. If these people don't exist in your life, you can also name a private fiduciary. You can also name multiple people for checks and balances or a private fiduciary to oversee. Armed with this knowledge, we were able to quickly identify people Greg and Alyson trusted.

Financial Education for Children

Many Americans spend their inheritances at a stunning rate. A 2015 study based on survey data from the Federal Reserve and a National Longitudinal Survey funded by the Bureau of Labor Statistics found that one-third of heirs had negative savings within two years of the gift.

Regardless of the size of monetary gift passed down to descendants, the key to a successful inheritance appears to be this: *parents must pass on a legacy of more than just money.*

How parents pass on their wealth to their children impacts whether a family legacy will only last a few years or for generations well beyond.

In the Instructions to Guardian Memorandum discussed above, you can recommend ways for the guardian you have appointed to teach your children the value of money and your values.

While preparing the memorandum is an excellent first step, the best time to teach your children about money as the eventual stewards of your family legacy is now, during their childhood, and continuing as they grow into adulthood. Unfortunately, a recent study of American families discovered that while parents have every intention of transferring their knowledge to their children, the majority of parents procrastinate educating their children until it's too late.

The RBC Wealth Management study discovered many barriers preventing parents from communicating their wishes to their children: 31% cite their own lack of preparedness as the main conversation barrier; 27% of respondents "don't believe inheritors are old enough"; 15% "don't believe they're ready"; and 13% are "not comfortable talking about their own death."

Both informal education guided by family and formal education through structural financial literacy programs is effective. Four out of five adult children surveyed reported that structured financial literacy programs made them feel more financially confident and prepared.

FINANCIAL EDUCATION AND LITERACY

Financial literacy and education with your children should include both general financial topics that everyone needs to know (i.e., creating a budget, savings and balancing a checkbook) and financial topics specific to your wealth (i.e., real estate investing and stock investing).

The following are financial education topics based on your child's age:

Pre-schoolers, First and Second Grade

1) Earning Money through allowance. Children learn that money isn't free. Children do certain tasks around the

home as a family member. Children are also given the opportunity to do additional bonus tasks and earn an allowance.

2) Spending plans and goal setting. Teach your children they can create goals for their money through a spending plan. They can either save the money, spend it or share it. When they get older expand to other options including investing.

Grades 3- 6

1) Money and Responsibility - responsible money management starts with keeping records of what is spent and what is saved. Teach your children how to track their purchases and savings.

2) Investing - teaching your kids about interest rates and investing in stocks. Purchase a stock from a company your child knows and have them track it over a time period.

3) Needs versus Wants - help your child understand the difference between needs and wants. Walk around the house and have your child categorize things as needs versus wants.

4) Sharing - teach your child about sharing through donating to causes and charities or doing fundraising activities. Have them choose a charity and follow how the funds help people.

Teens

1) Budgeting - help your teen understand how much money they need for a car, car insurance, gas and other expenses. Teach them about budgeting and cashflow.

2) Investing - help older children understand more advanced investing topics like market volatility and asset diversification. Set up a custodial brokerage account and teach them how to invest.

3) Family Business - if you have a family business, get them involved with different parts of the business.

Early adulthood:

1) Investments - parents should give their children more advanced education around investments and retirement planning.
2) Other topics specific to your family. Parents should involve children in annual meetings with financial advisor, CPA and attorneys.

In Chapter 7, we will discuss passing on your intangible assets, values, insights, and stories.

How can parents today better prepare themselves to preserve their legacies for generations to come? Parents should consider avoiding the pitfalls that research has shown by financially educating their children early and incorporating structured financial education programs. A list of financial education resources is available in the appendix and at LegallyEverAfter.com/Resources.

For those parents who get it right, they will raise their children's confidence levels, transfer vital knowledge, gain peace of mind and ensure that family legacies will last for future generations.

**Check out your free companion
course for added support and bonuses:**
LegallyEverAfter.com/Resources

5

A - ASSET PROTECTION: PLANNING FOR WEALTH PRESERVATION

"But like all dreams, I'm afraid this won't last forever."

—*Fairy Godmother*

Y ou have worked hard for your assets, and you should not have to fear that courts or creditors will take your assets away before your family can receive the benefits your assets can provide. Asset protection is a crucial part of legal and financial planning. Asset Protection avoids loss of your family's assets both during life and after you die. Assets include real estate, bank accounts, vehicles, and other types of property.

Creditors include frivolous lawsuits, credit card companies, banks, people who are filing and ex-spouses. All of these categories of creditors need to be planned for when setting up asset protection strategies.

Asset protection involves structuring a plan to keep funds out of the hands of fraudulent creditors and also prevents your assets from being stuck in probate court. When probate courts get involved, money is often lost that should go directly to the surviving family.

Protecting your assets is a matter of being intentional in how you manage your assets while you are alive and communicating clearly how you want your assets distributed upon your death.

7 TIPS FOR ASSET PROTECTION & WEALTH PRESERVATION

Asset protection helps families with larger financial assets but can be used by families with a lower net worth as well. The following are tips for Asset Protection:

1. Avoid a fraudulent conveyance (aka fraudulent transfer in some states).

Asset protection seems like major overkill until you actually need it. However, if you wait until harm arises, it is too late.

The timing of asset protection is important. The first concern is to never defraud your creditors. This type of planning should never start after you've been served with a lawsuit or a harm has been done. By that point, it is a *fraudulent* transfer if your property is transferred in a manner intended to defraud creditors, which could lead to criminal penalties, and all kinds of other things that can go wrong.

Claire's Bicycle Crash

I represented Claire, a client, who was riding with a group of cyclists going through a green light when a woman named Samantha ran the red light and crashed into them. Claire was seriously injured. Claire lost a limb, and she would have years of expensive surgeries and pain ahead of her. When the police arrived, Claire and the group explained they had the green light. Samantha also told the police she had the green light. The police could not determine who was telling the truth. Two days after the crash, Samantha transferred her $600,000 house to her sister for $10.

Due to the timing of the transfer, in addition to bringing claims against Samantha for the crash, we were able to bring claims against her for the transfer of the house; we argued it was a fraudulent conveyance. A fraudulent conveyance is defined as a transfer of property that is made to swindle, hinder, or delay a creditor, or to put such property beyond his or her reach. At trial, we were able to present the jury with the evidence of Claire's transfer to show consciousness of guilt. The jury ultimately believed our client and awarded her millions of dollars.

2. Obtain Proper Insurance & Work With a Trusted Advisor

Daycare Injury

I represented parents whose child was badly injured at a small family-owned daycare. The daycare business had an insurance policy but they hadn't read the language carefully. They chose the cheap policy and cut corners, not really understanding the risk they were taking on. Buried in the large policy was an exclusion for common injuries. As a result, the daycare owners had to pay for the child's injuries out of their own pocket, costing them hundreds of thousands of dollars. If they had just paid a few extra dollars a month for extra coverage, they would have had the insurance to cover our client's injuries.

Asset protection planning should never be a substitute for quality insurance. Comprehensive insurance is always the first layer of protection you should have in place. Consider obtaining property and casualty insurance, liability umbrella policies, commercial insurance, disability insurance, life insurance, professional and malpractice insurance.

Having the right carriers, the right coverages and the right amounts in place are going to ensure that first line of defense so that if you are sued or injured, the insurance is going to step in to help protect those assets you've worked hard to create.

I recommend working with a trusted insurance advisor to get the right coverages in place. When working with an insurance advisor, speak with them about the type of assets you have and the potential risks. Then go over all of the exclusions, the things not covered in the policy. Inquire if you can get coverage or a rider for those exclusions, and what the costs are. The biggest mistake I see is people getting a $1M Umbrella policy and thinking they are fully covered, but they actually have a false sense of security. Those exclusions are the holes in the umbrella and there are often affordable riders to fill in those gaps.

If your state has underinsured & uninsured motorist coverage, invest in the largest coverage you can afford. This coverage protects you if your family is hurt in a crash by someone who has no insurance or the minimum insurance policy (some states only require $15,000 of liability coverage for drivers). For example, I was contacted by a woman who was driving with her family and was T-boned by an uninsured driver. The uninsured driver had no insurance and no assets. This client didn't have uninsured motorist coverage, and the car crash nearly bankrupted her. She was out of work for over a year as a result of the crash and there was no way to compensate her. She wished she had spent just a few dollars more per month for uninsured motorist coverage, which would have compensated her and her family for the crash.

3. Start Simple and Utilize Exempt Assets.

I recently received a call from a recent medical school graduate who wanted to set up an offshore asset protection trust after watching a YouTube video. Offshore Asset protection trusts are costly, expensive to maintain and are definitely not the right solution for everyone. I discovered that the bulk of his assets were in a retirement plan which is already protected from creditors.

The old adage of walking before you run is true for asset protection. In most states, there are assets that through their very nature have protection from creditors. Examples include certain types of retirement plans, life insurance, and annuities. Also, in some states, the house you live in is protected. This is a way for you to invest and allocate your assets that have long term asset protection.

4. Use of Limited Liability Entities.

Creating limited liability companies or other corporate forms to house assets can work to help you protect those assets. If a liability exposure comes out of the business activity in that entity, you can trap those liabilities and protect them from spilling over into your other personal assets.

5. Living Trusts and Domestic asset protection trusts.

Living Trusts allow you to protect assets and minimize estate taxes at the death of you or your spouse, and after the second of you passes. Living Trusts, if drafted properly and funded correctly, will avoid the probate process. Some states like Wyoming, Nevada, Michigan and Ohio allow for creation of a domestic asset protection trust ("DAPT"). With a DAPT, you can create a trust to hold assets, still have access to those assets, but can prevent your creditors from being able to reach what's inside the DAPT. These types of trusts are complex and have to be set up properly, well in advance of any creditor problems.

6. Assemble the Right Team of Advisors

They will help you put into place your asset protection plan. Having Attorneys, CPAs, Financial Advisors and Insurance Brokers specialized in Asset Protection will ensure you are fully protected.

7. Lifetime Asset Protection for Your Children & Grandchildren

Lifetime Asset Protection Trusts, also known as Dynasty Trusts, protect your children from the scenarios above. Instead of your children receiving their inheritance outright, making the funds subject to future creditors and divorces, they receive their inheritance in an asset protection trust. You set the terms of the asset protection trust, and the limits. You can put more protection in place, or less, depending on the needs of your child.

For example, if your child has an addiction to drugs, alcohol or gambling now or in the future, you can put protections in place for someone else to be the steward of the money. Additionally, if your child is not good with money, you can appoint a co-trustee to guide their financial decisions.

Charlie's Lost Gift

Charlie's grandfather decided to purchase a house for Charlie and his parents to live in, and put the title in Charlie's parent's names. Charlie's grandfather's hope was for the house to be an asset that Charlie would inherit someday.

Unfortunately, Charlie's mother passed away unexpectedly and when Charlie's father remarried he never set up an estate plan. Several years later, Charlie's father also passed away and the house passed to Charlie's step mother.

Charlie's grandfather was upset, this house was supposed to pass to Charlie and now was outside the family with Charlie's estranged stepmother.

Carol's Divorce Loss

Carol inherited $300,000 from her parents when they passed away. At the time Carol was married to an abusive man. Several years later she finally divorced the man, but had to give $150,000 of her parents hard-earned money to her ex-husband.

Two Brothers

Carl and Gary are brothers that each received $500,000 from their parents after they died. Carl invested the money, and has over $2 Million set aside for his retirement and his grandchild's college fund. Gary spent all of his share in the first year on a new car, travel and miscellaneous consumer products. He is struggling financially and does not have enough money to retire.

BUSINESS PROTECTION

I represented a client who was a bystander in a bar fight. A glass meant to hit someone else injured him. The insurance policy for the bar would not cover bar fight and so I had to evaluate if the business owner's personal assets would have to pay for this business liability.

We discovered that the bar owner intermingled funds between his business and personal accounts. We also discovered that the bar owner did not properly operate and maintain his business entity and we had a strong argument to "pierce the corporate veil" and access his personal assets.

If the business owner had properly maintained his business entity, there would have been a legal barrier preventing us from collecting from his personal and other business assets. A business entity that is properly created, maintained and operated creates a legal barrier between business liability and your personal assets.

Small businesses should operate in the form of a limited liability entity (an "LLE"). Common forms of the LLE are limited liability companies (LLCs), corporations and limited partnerships. The available forms of LLE's for small business owners vary per state.

An LLE provides that the owners of the business can protect their personal assets from claims brought by the LLE's creditors. This protection is often referred to as the "corporate veil." For example, if a real estate investor purchases a piece of real estate in an LLC, and later there is a fire on the property and the LLC is sued, his personal assets should be protected. There are two ways that a creditor or injured party can get around or "pierce" the corporate veil.

1. If an owner or manager of the LLE is personally responsible for the act that results in a loss or harm to the creditor. For example, if the Owner of a construction company runs a red light and crashes a company vehicle, he is still personally liable for running the red light. He doesn't

avoid personal liability even though he was driving for a business purpose on company time.

2. The LLE is not properly operated and maintained by the owner as a business separate from himself or herself.

Proper operation and maintenance of a LLE depends on state specific laws, and your specific industries regulations.

The following is a general list of guidelines to properly operate and maintain an LLE. It is prudent to work with an experienced Business Attorney to comply with your state's specific laws.

1. Do not commingle personal and business finances. Never pay personal expenses with business funds, or vice versa. To accomplish this, the best practice is to have a separate business bank account for each business and a separate personal bank account.

2. Execute and sign business contracts in your representative capacity. For example, sign as Jane Doe, President of Doe Corporation. Do not sign the contract personally as Jane Doe.

3. Create and maintain a company record book, which should include records of all company meetings. For corporations, hold annual meetings for shareholders to elect directors and for directors to select officers.

4. Create and maintain company documents. For example, for an LLC, maintain an operating agreement. For a corporation, maintain articles of incorporation, bylaws and stock ownership ledger.

5. Register all business names with the Secretary of state and file the required annual, biannual or monthly, reports. If you operate in multiple states, register with each state.

6. Follow any requirements unique to the state and the industry where your business operates.

Estate Tax Minimization

According to the IRS, "the Estate Tax is a tax on your right to transfer property at your death." It includes the accounting of everything you own and certain interests at the date of your death. The fair market value of these items is used to value your estate at death. Your "gross estate" is the total value of all of these items which includes cash, real estate, securities, annuities, business interests and other assets.

Once you have accounted for the Gross Estate, certain deductions (and in special circumstances, reductions to value) are allowed in arriving at your "Taxable Estate." These deductions may include mortgages and other debts, estate administration expenses, property that passes to surviving spouses and qualified charities. The tax is then reduced by the available unified credit.

In simple terms, if your taxable estate is over the credit amount, you will be paying federal taxes. As of 2021, that tax rate is 40%. Both the credit amount and the tax rate depend on who is in power, and we don't know who will be in power when you pass away. In 2004, estates over $1.5 Million paid estate taxes. In 2012 estates over $5.1 Million paid estate taxes. In 2018 the taxable estate went up to $11.18 Million, which means only estates over that amount.

As of 2021, there are seven common ways high net worth families minimize estate tax exposure. However, there are proposals by the Biden administration to eliminate or reduce the availability of these strategies. If you have a net worth high enough to be impacted by estate tax law changes, it is a good idea to work with an attorney and tax professional to strategize and track changes.

The most common estate tax minimization strategies currently used as of November 2021, but potentially subject to change by a new administration are as follows:

1. Gifting to family members over their lifetime. For tax year 2021, you can give any one person up to $15,000 tax-free (or up to $30,000 if you're married and you're filing

joint tax returns). There is a cap of the lifetime gift you can give. In 2021, that lifetime cap is at an all-time high of $11.7 million of your wealth as gifts before getting hit with the gift tax. However the Biden administration has proposed reducing that amount significantly.

2. Irrevocable Life Insurance Trusts
3. Qualified Personal Residence Trusts
4. Charitable Donations
5. Family Limited Partnerships
6. Spousal Lifetime Access Trusts
7. Domestic Asset Protection Trusts and Hybrid Domestic Asset Protection Trusts

Tax minimization strategies are extremely complex, and the laws change frequently. Rely on your legal professional and tax professional to make sure that you are kept up-to-date on all of the changes and pending changes.

In addition to federal estate taxes, 17 states also have state estate or inheritance taxes. As of 2021, state inheritance or estate taxes are as follows according to the Tax Foundation.

- District of Columbia: Estate tax of 11.2 percent to 16 percent on estates above $4 million
- Hawaii: Estate tax of 10 percent to 20 percent on estates above $5.5 million
- Illinois: Estate tax of 0.8 percent to 16 percent on estates above $4 million
- Iowa: Inheritance tax of up to 15 percent
- Kentucky: Inheritance tax of up to 16 percent
- Maine: Estate tax of 8 percent to 12 percent on estates above $5.8 million
- Maryland: Estate tax of 0.8 percent to 16 percent on estates above $5 million; inheritance tax of up to 10 percent
- Massachusetts: 0.8 percent to 16 percent on estates above $1 million

- Minnesota: 13 percent to 16 percent on estates above $3 million
- Nebraska: Inheritance tax of up to 18 percent
- New Jersey: Inheritance tax of up to 16 percent
- New York: Estate tax of 3.06 percent to 16 percent for estates above $5.9 million
- Oregon: Estate tax of 10 percent to 16 percent on estates above $1 million
- Pennsylvania: Inheritance tax of up to 15 percent
- Rhode Island: Estate tax of 0.8 percent to 16 percent on estates above $1.6 million
- Vermont: Estate tax of 16 percent on estates above $5 million
- Washington: Estate tax of 10 percent to 20 percent on estates above $2.2 million

Check out your free companion course for added support and bonuses:
LegallyEverAfter.com/Resources

6

C - CARRY THROUGH, COMMUNICATE & UPDATE

"They can't order me to stop dreaming."

—Cinderella

Once you create an estate plan, you need to carry through, communicate and be sure you notify your trusted guardians and trustees of all your plans. They need to know where your original documents are, and which documents should be used in what situations. Your plan also needs to be updated throughout your life as circumstances change. If you have minor children, you want to give your guardianship documents and wishes to the guardians you have selected. A plan only works if people know it exists and where it is.

STORING ESTATE PLANNING DOCUMENTS

Grandmother's Flood

Melissa's mom passed away in childbirth, and her father was a drug addict. Melissa was raised by her grandmother.

Melissa's grandmother prepared a will leaving everything to Melissa and her great grandchildren and disinheriting her estranged son. Melissa received copies of the will. However, Melissa never knew where her grandmother kept the originals. Melissa took care of her grandmother in her later years and they shared a special bond. Melissa's father was estranged from the family, and neither she nor her grandmother heard from him for 30 years. Melissa's grandmother passed away and Melissa could not locate the original will.

Melissa remembered her grandmother's home flooded, and she figured out that the water damage destroyed the original documents. After her grandmother's death, her father sought to inherit the estate. Melissa consulted with several lawyers whom all agreed it wasn't worth litigating, as her father would inherit the estate. Without the originals, it would be treated as though the will did not exist, and the court would recognize her father as the heir and it would entitle him to receive 100 percent of the estate. Melissa reluctantly agreed not to pursue legal action.

Safely securing your original estate planning documents is critical. If the original documents are lost, stolen, or damaged beyond recognition, your plan may be completely invalidated. The following are options for safely securing your estate planning documents.

1. **Home storage.** If you decide to secure your original estate planning documents, the best practice is to store them in a waterproof and fireproof safe or bag. The safe will protect the documents from theft. If you choose home storage, be sure your trustees know where the documents are stored in your home and are given instructions to gain access if locked.

2. **Safety Deposit box.** Estate planning documents can be stored in a safety deposit box at a bank. It is important that your trustees know which bank they are stored at and can gain access upon your death or disability. Be sure to

review the policies with the bank you chose. Some banks require a court order for access after you die.

3. **Storing Originals with an Attorney.** In some states, attorneys will store originals or duplicate originals of your estate planning documents.

4. **Corporate fiduciary.** If you have named a bank or trust company as a trustee or executor, they can store your original estate planning documents for you.

In order to ensure emergency access to copies of your plan, I recommend a subscription to a third-party online storage service. To ensure emergency access to copies of your plan, consider using an online service like My Life and Wishes. While access to original documents is critical, having copies safely accessible to your loved ones is also vital.

Filing of Estate Planning Documents

While you are living, you can keep your estate planning documents private and most states do not require you to publicly file the documents. If you create a Living trust, that stays private upon your death. The probate court does not become involved with Living Trust plans.

However, if you create a will, when you pass away most states require your will to be publicly filed promptly. Once a will is filed, it's a matter of public record and anyone can view it. This is why celebrities' wills show up quickly online.

For example, Marilyn Monroe's will left her belongings to her acting coach Lee Strasberg with instructions to distribute to her friends and family. Strasberg kept all of Monroe's belongings in storage instead. Strasberg's widow auctioned off Monroe's belongings after his death and eventually made $13.4 Million.

Update your Asset Inventory

Erica's Father

Erica's father died unexpectedly. When he died, Erica knew nothing about his finances. Her parents divorced over 15 years earlier, and her mom tried to help her figure out where his assets might be but fell short. Erica felt like she had to become a private investigator; it took her over a year to locate her father's assets. She is now in the third year of probate on his estate. Erica described the whole process as exhausting and frustrating. The mess she had to clean up also caused a strain in her relationship with her siblings, who did not want to help her sort through things but also were impatiently waiting for their inheritance. After going through the process for her father, it motivated her to put together an estate plan so her husband and children would never suffer the way she had.

One of the biggest risks to your family's financial well-being is them not knowing what assets you have and where they are if something were to happen to you. For example, if you and your partner were to die today, would your family be able to find all of your assets, including bank accounts, insurance accounts, and investments? The reality is they would not. The California Department of Unclaimed Property has over $9 Billion in unclaimed assets.

Put together a folder or a spreadsheet of all of your assets, including account numbers and institutions, and keep that with your estate plan.

Updating Your Estate Plan

Review your plan at regular intervals in addition to major life events to help ensure that your legacy, both financial and otherwise, is passed on in accordance with your wishes and that your beneficiaries receive their benefits as smoothly as possible.

How often you need to update your estate plan really depends on the dynamics involved with your estate. I usually tell folks, if they have major life changes, it's a good time to check in. All of my plans are written to include future born children, but I have clients who have come to me who did an estate plan with another lawyer 20 years ago. And a lot changes in 20 years. For example, your children grow up and you want them to have more financial control. You may also have different people that you would want to be involved in your plan.

Real estate investors and business owners typically need to update their estate plan more frequently.

Typically, you should update an estate plan when major life changes occur.

Many people review their estate plan at a regular frequency, often when they review their whole financial plan. This can be done annually, semi-annually, or quarterly; for estate planning specifically, the general recommendation is at least every three to five years or when there is a life event. You may want to get your attorney or tax advisor's help.

In addition to regular reviews, it's a good idea to review and update your plan at life events like the following:

- The birth or adoption of a new child or grandchild
- When a child or grandchild becomes an adult
- When a child or grandchild needs educational funding
- Death or change in circumstances of the guardian named in your will for minor children
- Changes in your number of dependents, such as the addition of caring for an adult
- Change in your or your spouse's financial or other goals
- Marriage or divorce
- Illness or disability of your spouse
- Change in your life or long-term care insurance coverage
- Purchasing a home or other large asset
- Borrowing a large amount of money or taking on liability for any other reason

- Large increases or decreases in the value of assets, such as investments
- If you or your spouse receives a large inheritance or gift
- Changes in federal or state laws covering taxes and investments
- If any family member passes away, becomes ill, or becomes disabled
- Death or change in circumstance of your executor or trustee
- Career changes, such as a new job, promotion, or if you start or close a business

DIGITAL ASSETS

Recent advances in digital technology have resulted in many of us collecting and storing digital assets. Without proper estate planning, locating and accessing digital assets after we die can be a major challenge for our loved ones.

Two Types of Digital Assets

Generally, there are two types of digital assets that should be planned for in your estate plan: assets with financial value and assets with sentimental value.

Financial Digital Assets: Digital assets with financial value include NFTs, CryptoCurrency, Online payment accounts (i.e. Venmo), loyalty programs (i.e. frequent flyer miles) as well as revenue generating digital assets like blogs and intellectual property.

Sentimental assets: Sentimental digital assets have little or no financial value but a significant sentimental value. These are things like social media accounts, apps, photo storage sites and email accounts.

Is the asset transferrable?

Whether the asset is transferable upon your death depends on the type of licenses you have. For example, cryptocurrency and PayPal accounts can be transferred upon death in an estate plan. However, your kindle e-book collection is not transferable upon death. The type of license you have is usually spelled out in the Terms of Service Agreement.

While you can provide your loved ones account login and passwords, this may violate the Terms of Service Agreement and privacy laws.

The majority of states have adopted laws to clarify how digital assets can be accessed and disposed of in the event of your death or incapacity.

3 Steps for Including Digital Assets in Your Estate Plan

Follow these three steps to ensure that your digital assets are properly passed on:

1. Create a List of Your Digital Assets: Begin by creating a list of all the digital assets you currently own. Provide instructions and passwords for accessing each asset. Consider using a password management app, such as LastPass, to simplify this effort and keep things updated throughout your life.

If you own cryptocurrency, prepare detailed instructions about how to access your cryptocurrency, and ensure that one or more people you trust know that you have a cryptocurrency and how to find your instructions.

2. Understand what you really own. Review the terms of service for each of your assets to determine what you really own and confirm you, in fact, have a transferable license. If the license is not transferable, remove it from the inventory. Check to see if the asset has tools for you to designate someone in the event of your death. For example, Facebook has tools for you to designate people to manage your account after your death.

3. Include your digital assets in your estate plan: Once you've created your inventory of digital assets, you'll need to add those assets to your estate plan. Never include specific passwords and accounts in estate planning documents which can be easily read by others. This is very important for wills which become a public record upon your death. Keep the password information stored in a secure place and let your fiduciary know how to find and use it.

**Check out your free companion
course for added support and bonuses:**
LegallyEverAfter.com/Resources

7

Y - YOUR FAMILY LEGACY

"Perhaps the greatest risk any of us will ever
take is to be seen as we really are. "

—*Cinderella*

The greatest wealth transfer in history is happening now. Approximately $70 trillion will be transferred down between 2018 and 2042, according to Cerulli Associates. How parents pass on their estate affects whether a family legacy will last only a few years or create a lasting legacy for generations to come.

Parents often focus most of their attention on the technical tools to preserve and pass on their wealth to the next generation. While these tools are important, we know when you are gone, your children are not going to hold your living trust documents when they miss you. Your children are going to need more to remember you by.

Further, as we discussed in Chapter 4, Americans spend their inheritance at an alarming rate and financially educating children is important for a successful inheritance. 70% of wealthy families lose their wealth by the second generation, and 90% by the third, according to the Williams Group wealth consultancy.

In addition to financial education, passing on values, insights and stories appears to be just as important. Unfortunately, many of us procrastinate capturing these intangible assets until it's too late.

There are three keys to successful wealth transfer and a lasting family legacy:

1. Financial education and literacy (discussed in Chapter 4)
2. Passing on values, insights and stories
3. Intentional communication.

PASSING ON FAMILY VALUES, INSIGHTS AND STORIES

Growing up, my family had an annual New Year's Eve tradition. Every year, my father asked us to share our goals for the coming year, and he wrote them down. These new year's goal-writing sessions and regular check-ins with my father were part of something bigger. An unspoken family mission in our family was achieving goals and supporting our family members to achieve their goals. You likely have an unspoken family mission statement as well.

Many family's first mission statements are their wedding vows.

Taking the time to create a family mission statement fosters a positive family culture. Building a healthy, loving and safe family culture doesn't happen by default. It requires parents to be intentional, and to set a pathway for children with a vision. A family mission statement helps children feel like they are part of something bigger than themselves, creates a strong family connection and ultimately builds confidence, resilience and healthy self-esteem.

Why Create a Family Mission Statement?

A family mission statement creates a shared vision, values and purpose which bonds a family together. It helps parents and children feel connected and creates a sense of purpose and belonging.

What exactly is a Family Mission Statement?

A family mission statement lays out your family's purpose, goals and standards.

In 1989, Stephen Covey, wrote a book called *7 Habits of Highly Effective Families*. Covey, a Harvard-trained business consultant, often asked his clients to write one sentence mission statements about their purpose and realized mission statements were just as important for families.

Your family mission statement keeps your family on track to achieve your goals.

How to Create a Family Mission Statement

Before you begin creating your family mission statement, keep in mind the process is more important than the end result. The goal here isn't to have a statement that "looks right" or checks all the boxes. The magic and connection happens when you intentionally take the time to connect as a family.

Create an environment where each member of the family shares and everyone listens. Just the simple act of listening and affirming each child and your partner's hopes, values and dreams increases connection and confidence. Remember, discussing what it means to live a good life is a lifelong discussion. The important thing is that you start the conversation.

Step 1: Schedule a special family meeting, make it fun and age appropriate.

Schedule a special family meeting and include all members of the family. The goal is to create a fun and special environment to connect as a family. You can order a special meal at home, set up the bonfire outside or go for a family hike. This shouldn't seem like a chore and should be arranged to be fun for everyone involved. Remember, kids of all ages have varying attention spans. If you have younger kids between 4-10, keep discussions to

15-30 minutes. For older kids, 30-45 minutes may work best. Don't rush the process, it can be stretched over multiple meetings.

Step 2: Ask questions and discuss.

Give your spouse and children the opportunity to express and be heard. Consider asking the following questions:

1. What is the purpose of our family?
2. What things do we want to do?
3. What type of relationships do we want with each other and others?
4. What kind of feelings do we want in our home?
5. What kind of home do you want to invite your friends to?
6. What are our family's priorities?
7. What are our responsibilities as family members?
8. How can we contribute to our community?
9. Who are our heroes and what aspects would we like to emulate?
10. What brings us joy?
11. What legacy do we want to leave?

Take the time to listen, reflect and write down every family member's contributions.

Example of Core Family Values:

Always continue to learn
Learn from failures
Show love daily
Be honest
Have fun
Never give up
Take personal responsibility
Be kind
Be adventurous and creative
Do more with less

Step 3: Agree on the main points.

You've now collected a large list of your family's values, goals and ideas. It's time to narrow down to the top 5-10.

To narrow the list down, consider going through and starring the goals and values that more than one family member has suggested. You can also give each family member 4 votes, and narrow down the list from there.

Whichever technique you use to prioritize the list, be sure to connect and give every family member a voice in the process.

Step 4: Write your Mission Statement.

Now that you have a list of the top 5-10 values of your family, it is time to draft your mission statement.

Your final mission statement can be in the form of a bulleted list, or in the form of a sentence or even a song.

You can take inspiration from business, nonprofit and personal mission statements.

Examples of business and nonprofit mission statements:

"Bring inspiration and innovation to every athlete in the world.*

*If you have a body, you are an athlete." —Nike

"To inspire and nurture the human spirit—one person, one cup, and one neighborhood at a time." —Starbucks

"To Bring Safe Water & Sanitation to the World" —Water.org

Examples of personal mission statements of successful people:

"To be a teacher. And to be known for inspiring my students to be more than they thought they could be." —Oprah Winfrey

"My mission in life is not merely to survive, but to thrive; and to do so with some passion, some compassion, some humor, and some style." —Maya Angelou

"To have fun in my journey through life and learn from my mistakes." —*Richard Branson*

Example Family Mission Statement

In our family we:

- Have fun
- Show our love
- Appreciate each other
- Are honest
- Make the world a better place

Step 5: Display your Family Mission Statement.

Once you have finalized your mission statement, consider creating a poster or sign together. Display your mission statement somewhere in your home. Displaying your mission statement in a prominent area of your home will provide a daily reminder and foster a sense of belonging and community.

Step 6: Review and update your mission statement.

Your mission statement will change and grow with your family. Consider updating it as often as your family's life changes; for example, with the addition of new family members or when your children reach new milestones (i.e., graduate from elementary school).

LOVE LETTERS & LEGACY INTERVIEWS

My grandfather passed away suddenly and I would have loved to have something to remember him by, such as a recording or a letter.

Putting together your legacy, your stories and insights, is a really beautiful gift you can give to your loved ones. We do a process at my law firm called a legacy interview, where we give you specific questions to record for your loved ones on different topics, so that you can really start preparing for this. For those that are camera shy, writing legacy letters is also effective.

Take the time to write or record a legacy love letter to your child, spouse, or another loved one by following these steps:

Legacy Love Letter or Recording 10-Minute Exercise

1. Choose the person who will receive the letter or recording.
2. Set a timer for 10 minutes. If you are recording, imagine the person is sitting in front of you before looking into the camera or starting the audio recording.
3. Answer as many of these questions and prompts as you can or desire in the ten minutes.
    i.   Some things I love most about you are . . .
    ii. My hopes and dreams for your future are . . .
    iii. How I felt the day you were born or the day I met you . . .
    iv. Thank you for . . .
    v.   Please forgive me for . . .
    vi. You have made me a better person by . . .
    vii. My advice for you on hard days . . .
    viii. My advice for you in your life . . .
    ix. What I want you to remember about me . . .
    x.   If I could be with you right now I would want you to know . . .
    xi. Some memories of you that I'd like to share . . .
    xii. Anything that has been left unsaid, share it . . .
4. You can share the letter with them now, or put it in a safe place that they will know about. For my clients, my office provides an estate planning binder with a section to include these letters.

Excerpt from Letter to My Daughter

Dear Daughter,

Today I'm leaving for my first trip away from you since you were born 9 months ago. I know I will be home in a few days, but I wanted to take this moment to tell you how much I love you.

From the moment you were born, I knew you were special. You were so curious and alert from the first moment in my arms.

Over the past 9 months, you continue to amaze me each day. These past 9 months being your mom have been the happiest of my life. I am so grateful and happy to be your mom.

When I was a little girl my father, your grandfather, taught me a few things I hope to teach you.

1. *Dream big, you can accomplish anything you set your mind to.*
2. *Be kind to others, treat them as you want to be treated.*
3. *Make the world a better place.*

When in doubt, follow your heart.
I believe in you. I am proud of you. I love you.

Love,
Mom

INTENTIONAL COMMUNICATION

Three Sons

Tony owned three restaurants he wanted to pass on to his son Leo. Leo had always worked hard in the business and he was the natural choice. Tony's other sons, Robert and Vince, had pursued other careers. Tony didn't think his choice would be an issue with his children and seemed obvious. However, when Tony and I met, I encouraged him to have a conversation with his adult children about the plan we designed together. I told Tony about similar cases where, after the parents passed, siblings fought about ongoing management of the family business and assumptions about their parents' wishes. I also encouraged him to set up a family meeting for us to go over the plan together with his children, so everyone would be on the same page and to minimize the risk of future litigation. To Tony's surprise, Leo did not want to carry on the family business alone, he wanted support from his brothers. The brothers appreciated Leo's desire to involve them, but they didn't share wanting input. Together the family was able to frankly discuss the future, while everyone was healthy and no one was making assumptions. These short meetings brought the family together and gave Tony and his kids the peace of mind that the family wealth would transition smoothly.

Many parents fear talking about their finances and estate plan with their children. Part of this fear stems from worries that these conversations will lead to entitled children who lack motivation. Instead, parents want to foster independence and self-confidence and mistakenly avoid the opportunity to talk about their plans for the family after their death. Parents want their children to succeed in life, work and their relationships. Some parents worry about future divorces, and don't want in-law children to know about their wealth. Additionally, thinking and speaking about death can be uncomfortable.

The truth is, secrecy about wealth, legacy and estate planning often leads to confusion and problems for those left behind when you die. Communication isn't easy, but the alternative is much worse. If your children are minors, document these important topics in a memorandum and share with the financial guardians/trustees you have named.

Important Topics to Communicate

1. Values, Goals and Intentions with your Wealth

If you've set up a family mission statement (as discussed above), then communicating your values, goals and intention with your wealth should be a natural extension. If you haven't set up your family mission statement, start there. Look for ways to teach your children throughout the rest of your life. Don't just tell, show them. For example, some parents have their children invest and track stocks on graph paper from a young age. Other parents get their kids involved with managing their rental property.

2. Wealth Transfer Strategy

Your wealth transfer strategy will change over time. However, you should think about what your guidance and advice would be if something were to happen to you in the short-term. For example, if you own a large real estate investment portfolio, do you want that sold, or kept? Communicate that wish and the strategy behind it.

3. Estate Planning Document and Roles

Explain what documents you have, where they are stored, the roles and the reasons behind the roles.

4. Family Advisors

Share information about who your CPA, financial advisors, attorney and business advisors are.

5. Family Wealth Inventory

Share an inventory of all of your assets, and identify information for each.

6. Health Wishes

Explain your wishes if you become incapacitated.

Family Meeting

When I was in college, my parents updated their estate plan and mailed me a large envelope full of estate planning documents. I had no legal education at that point, and I didn't open the envelope. I shoved it in my closet. If my parents had been hospitalized, I would have had no idea what document to use or that I even had a document that I could use.

At my law firm, we offer family meetings to our clients with adult children. During this meeting, we go through the essential estate planning documents and I answer the children's legal questions and explain the documents. I also encourage my clients to set up subsequent family meetings to discuss their values, goals, wealth strategy, and family wealth inventory.

The family meetings you set up with your children should be positive and approachable experiences. You should be celebrating the success of passing on the wealth in your family. Successful family meetings should engage family members in open, healthy trust building conversations. These meetings shouldn't be a set of rules or one sided. Take the time to allow your children to digest information and ask questions.

Start these family meetings early and continue throughout adulthood.

Hiring a Professional to Facilitate or Lead

If you like the idea of creating a family mission and guiding your family legacy but would like professional help, consider bringing in an expert or team of experts.

Facilitating and Leading the Discussion

You can hire a religious leader (i.e. priest or rabbi), professional facilitator, therapist, life coach, life planner, financial advisor or attorney to help you facilitate and lead your family legacy discussions or parts of these discussions.

Check out your free companion course for added support and bonuses:
LegallyEverAfter.com/Resources

8

THE WAY TO CREATE A
LEGALLY PROTECTED PLAN

Family Business and Online Plans

*Tim and his father ran a successful construction company
together for many years. His 80-year-old father was ready to retire
and pass on the business to Tim. One night, Tim and his father
went online and drafted estate planning documents. A few years
later, Tim's father passed away. The estate plan Tim's father
drafted online failed. The online plan wasn't properly executed by
his father. His father did not understand how to pass on the business correctly, and instead of passing it on to Tim, it was now
split between Tim and his estranged and drug-addicted brother.*

*The business real estate holdings which Tim had contributed
financially to purchase were titled in his father's name solely.
Therefore, his brother now had a claim to them. For the next three
years, Tim spent countless hours and hundreds of thousands of
dollars in probate court battling with his estranged brother. Tim
had to take out a mortgage on his house to keep the business
afloat. Tim's marriage became strained. He barely had any time
to spend with his kids and he gained weight from the stresses of
the court process.*

Tim came to my office because he wanted to put together an estate plan to ensure that the nightmare he went through with his brother won't ever happen again. In four short weeks, we put together a comprehensive and personalized plan which will protect his children, keep them out of court, reduce taxes and eliminate the cost of probate.

Should you hire a lawyer to create a plan?

There are several do-it-yourself templates and online resources to help you create your own estate plan. Can you write your own estate plan? The simple answer is yes, you can write your own estate plan. However, the more important question is, should you write your own estate plan?

Many people feel tempted by the seemingly low cost of using an online legal document provider to create legal documents. However, doing so could result in your plan failing, not doing what you wanted it to do, and long-term costs for your loved ones.

Hiring an experienced lawyer to prepare your legal plan provides the following advantages:

1. An Estate planning lawyer will save you time, money, energy and will avoid common mistakes.

    Estate planning is complicated. Working with a legal professional helps. Hiring an estate planning lawyer will reduce the stress associated with securing your assets. One misplaced signature or omitted word can invalidate your estate plan.

    Common mistakes an estate planning lawyer can help you avoid include:

    · Designating incorrect beneficiaries on life insurance and retirement accounts
    · Not completing the process
    · Inadvertently leaving people out
    · Not including all of your assets

- Improper execution of documents
- Improper or inadequate funding of trusts

An estate planning lawyer will prevent mistakes and ensure you and your loved ones are cared for the way you intend. A carefully created plan will also help you protect your family from unnecessary conflict down the road.

2. Counseling
The "Simple Plan"

A New Jersey woman just needed a seemingly simple plan. She owned a $300,000 house and a $300,000 bank account. She had two adult children. She drafted a simple will herself, giving her house to her son and the bank account to her daughter. After her death, her children discovered her will and realized she's spent down her bank account to pay her bills, so there was nothing left for her daughter. The son who got the house felt sorry for his sister, but believed his mom wanted him to have the house. The daughter believed that was not her mother's intent and sued her brother. If the New Jersey mom would have had proper counseling and advice from a lawyer, the suit could have been avoided and her wishes would have been properly expressed in a legally binding document.

An estate planning lawyer provides more than technical document expertise. An estate planning lawyer is a trusted advisor who provides guidance, support and strategy.

For example, many parents struggle with deciding who they should designate as the ideal guardian for their child. An experienced estate planning lawyer will help a couple sift through the various options and choose a guardian based on their specific needs and circumstances.

3. Save Money on Taxes

    Prince's unexpected death in 2016 resulted in numerous court cases. Prince died without any estate planning documents. Prince did not have a spouse or children, and left behind half-brothers and half-sisters.

    The federal estate tax is 40 percent and Minnesota imposes a top death rate of 16 percent. There is a potential that Prince's $300 million estate will be reduced to $162 million just from taxes. This does not include the costs of probate, lawyers and litigation. Five years later, Prince's heirs still have not inherited a dime, and there are already over $13 million in attorneys fees.

    With some planning, Prince could have taken steps to keep his family members out of court and conflict and reduce estate taxes. Prince generously donated to charities. By failing to have an estate plan in place to continue those charitable gifts, Prince's estate lost out on the tremendous tax savings and the government, rather than the charities he supported, will benefit financially.

    State and federal tax laws often change and have become complicated. Many states have adopted their own estate tax structures.

    A qualified estate planning lawyer will stay up-to-date with these tax laws and help you prepare and update your plan to minimize taxes.

4. Updates

    Kobe Bryant's 7-month old daughter was left out of his estimated $600 million dollar estate. Although Bryant and his wife had an estate plan in place, the estate plan failed to name their youngest child, Capri Bryant. The Co-Trustees of the Kobe Bryant Trust filed a Petition to Modify Trust and add Capri as a beneficiary and luckily the petition was granted.

    However, the estate planning team made a major error by not updating the plan after Capri's birth or by not including future born children in the original plan. This mistake cost Kobe's wife Vanessa hefty sums of money to fix and it also eliminated the biggest benefits of the trust by exposing the estate details to the public and by not keeping his surviving family members out of court.

As Kobe's case shows, estate planning is not a one and done type of deal. Your plan must be updated as your life changes.

Births, deaths, marriages, divorces and incapacity alter a person's life. These life changes also impact the desired income of an estate plan. For example, in many states a divorce automatically invalidates prior Wills and other estate planning documents.

I recommend you review your plan every 3 years and immediately following life events to be sure your family is protected. Having a relationship with an attorney who has a process in place to easily allow for these reviews is key.

5. Complex Situations

Many people believe they have a simple situation and only need a simple will. However, as the New Jersey example demonstrated, simple can turn out to be unexpectedly complex.

If you are in a blended family, own a business, own real estate out of state, have a disabled family member, a special needs child, or are concerned about asset protection, an estate planning attorney will benefit everyone involved.

For example, when a person is special needs and requires governmental assistance, an inheritance may disqualify them from a critical service. Luckily, there are specific types of trust that can be set up for those with special needs, allowing them to continue to receive benefits and receive their inheritance. However, setting up a special needs trust is complex and specialized. It is important to work with an experienced estate planning attorney to properly protect special needs loved ones.

6. Objectivity

Norm and Paula have three adult children. Their youngest daughter is estranged from them, despite all of their efforts to reunite. They would like to disinherit their youngest daughter, but they worry about future unintended consequences if they decide to disinherit her.

The Wilsons love their family members, but in their heart if something were to happen to them they'd rather their good friends raise their kids. However, they worry about how their family will react to this.

Putting an estate plan in place can be an emotional process. Fear, doubt, and guilt can get in the way of making the right decision for you and your loved ones.

Estate planning lawyers can provide objectivity and help you navigate complex family dynamics and choose the best plan for your family.

FINDING THE RIGHT ATTORNEY

When you are researching estate planning attorneys, you can look online and you can also check with your friends, family and trusted advisors. Not all estate planning attorneys are equal. Below are key considerations for finding the right attorney.

1. **Avoid Hourly Fees or $399 Offers**

   Flat fees vs. Hourly Fees. The advantage of flat fees is everything is agreed to in advance and there are no surprises. It also encourages the attorney to be your advisor and develop a relationship. Beware of $399 Price Quotes from attorneys who don't take the time to understand your situation and speak with you. When I work with my clients, I do everything personalized. I don't do price quotes over the phone, because I want to be sure people aren't paying for things they don't need. If a law firm offers a low priced estate plan on their website, chances are they are doing a form document that won't be customized and personalized for you or there is an unseen cost on the back end. They are not going to take the time to be a true advisor and are instead going to give you a low-cost, low quality and quick solution.

A lawyer offering estate plans for $2,000 or less is usually cutting corners, churning through as many clients as possible and is undercutting their fees because they aren't providing much more than what you can download online. In ugly situations, they are selling you a high commissioned insurance product or luring you in with a low price offer and then upselling on the back end. Look for attorneys that really take the time to understand your assets, what you actually need, and to educate you.

When researching flat fees, ask the lawyer if:

- all the fees are flat fees, or are there other expenses?
- what happens if I call with a question after my plan is complete?
- how will you be sure my assets are owned the right way?
- how will you keep my plan up to date? how am I charged for this?

2. **Ask about support funding your trust.**

If you are setting up a living trust, transferring your assets into the trust correctly is vital. The process of transferring assets into your trust is known as "funding" your trust. If your assets aren't transferred to the trust correctly, then you just wasted your money on a stack of paper that isn't going to protect your family.

Be sure the firm will give you some type of support through the funding process.

At our firm, we provide unlimited guidance and support for funding your living trust, a full funding toolkit and a final review meeting to be sure things were transferred correctly.

3. **Ongoing Updates**. Ask the attorney how you can go about updating the trust throughout your life. Many estate plans fail because people forget to update their estate plans. I include a no-cost 3 year plan review with all of my clients. I also have a monthly newsletter updating my clients on any changes to estate planning laws. You want to be sure that the attorney and firm has a process for you to stay in touch if you need additional support.

4. **How long does creating an estate plan take?**

   Putting an estate plan in place takes time. How much time should you expect it to take from the time you hire an attorney until you sign your plan? I have heard horror stories of employees using prepaid legal planning law firms for estate plans and it took 1 year to get their estate plan from the lawyer.

   At our firm, our plans take between 4-to-6 weeks to prepare depending on the level of complexity. We also have expedited options for emergency and urgent situations.

5. **Boutique vs. Large Law Firms**

   Jane went to a large downtown law firm for her estate plan. At the initial meeting, the firm assured her she was making the right choice. At her follow-up meeting, she was assigned a recent law school graduate who couldn't answer her questions and rushed her through the process. The end result, she had no confidence in the plan that was created. She felt like it looked like something she could have created online and it wasn't worth the high price tag. A few weeks later when she met with her financial advisor and accountant, she discovered numerous errors that needed to be changed. At the recommendation of a colleague, Jane came to my office and I took the time to review the plan with her, modify the errors and help her understand how her goals could be achieved. We designed a new plan that actually met her needs and gave her full confidence.

Large law firms typically aren't designed to serve families under $100m. They save their best attorneys for high net worth cases and the rest get the recent grads. No one likes to feel like they aren't a priority and their matter is a training ground. Large law firms have high overhead, high billable hour requirements, high hourly fees and a business model that doesn't meet the needs of families with assets under $100m seeking a trusted advisor.

With a boutique law firm like ours, we specialize in filling this gap in the market. Our typical clients have under $100m in assets, and they are seeking quality services at a reasonable price. As a boutique law firm focused on estate planning, we don't have high overhead because we aren't covering the costs of a large downtown building covered in marble. We also aren't offsetting the costs of other departments, like litigation, which tends to have more peaks and valleys. We also limit the number of clients we take each month, so each client receives the highest quality and our undivided attention.

6. **Is the lawyer an expert in the kind of service you actually need?**

Bill grew up in a small mountain town. There was one lawyer in town who handled criminal matters, divorce matters, litigation matters and estate planning. He was a "take what comes in the door" kind of lawyer. The lawyer was smart. He knew a little about everything and a lot of about nothing.

When Bill's parents died, Bill ended up in probate court and spent hundreds of thousands of dollars. Bill's parents had a will created by the neighborhood lawyer. That will was useless. Bill asked the lawyer why he didn't set up a trust for his parents. The lawyer said, "I only do wills." Bill wondered why the lawyer didn't refer his parents to an estate planning attorney with specialized knowledge in the field.

Estate planning is complex and requires expertise. Unfortunately, there are many attorneys that advertise that they can create a will or estate plan. However, when you dig into their profile, you see that their experience and focus is elsewhere.

Many times these attorneys focus on another practice area like divorces or business law. They start to receive inquiries from their divorced clients to update their estate plan, and so they take a one hour class and start creating estate plans.

Unfortunately, their clients don't know any better. Many years later, I come across these families after the plans fail and the clean-up is expensive. You may be wondering how these attorneys get away with this. The attorneys don't know what they don't know. The attorneys aren't intentionally misleading their clients. They don't know advanced estate planning tools because they don't specialize in this area. Clients simply ask for a will because they don't know what they truly need. These lawyers are focused on the document instead of being a trust advisor, and they deliver the will as promised.

However, if they were experts in estate planning, they wouldn't have focused on the document and they would have taken a step back and understood the client's assets, goals and objectives.

Lawyers focused on estate planning are worth seeking out. They have invested the time and energy to deeply understand the legal, financial and tax implications of your estate and will be a trusted legal advisor. The strategy they design for you will be well worth the expense and effort.

Finally, Estate planning is a personal process that requires a relationship based on trust. Most lawyers will do a free consultation so you can really see if it's a good fit for both of you. Take that time, and confirm whether it feels like a good fit.

Holly's Story

Holly and her husband Sam just celebrated the birth of their third child and decided to set up an estate plan. They reached out to Sam's employer who offers a benefit of a free will with a local attorney through a prepaid legal services plan. The first opening was six months away, they took the appointment and in the meantime Holly researched estate planning options and became highly interested in setting up a living trust. When they came to the appointment the lawyer was unprepared, kept calling them by the wrong name and plugged their name into a word template that looked very similar to what they found online. When Holly asked about setting up a Living Trust, the lawyer told them it's not included in the free plan. When Holly asked about the pros/cons and what the price difference would be, the lawyer quoted her a high hourly rate and couldn't tell her how many hours it would take. The lawyer then spoke over their head using legal jargon. Frustrated and confused, Holly and Sam left with a form will, and wondered why they even bothered meeting with a lawyer.

A few weeks later, Sam and Holly were at a party with a friend who shared the positive experience she went through at our law firm. Sam and Holly called our office the next day, and were scheduled on my calendar three weeks later. When Sam, Holly and I met, I started with a family wealth planning session where I went through all of their assets, explained how everything should transfer, learned about their specific needs and designed an estate plan personalized to them. I took the time to explain everything and Holly and Sam felt empowered and educated. I quoted a one time flat fee, so there were no surprises. I walked them through our comprehensive process to ensure their plan will work for their loved ones and they left with the peace of mind knowing they are fully protected.

UNIQUE SITUATIONS IN ESTATE PLANNING

What if my Spouse is a Not a U.S. Citizen?

It is important to discuss the tax implications of planning for a foreign spouse living in the US. One tool for minimizing estate taxes if the US spouse dies and wishes to leave everything to the non-citizen spouse is a qualified domestic trust (QDOT). A qualified domestic trust is a specific trust that allows taxpayers who survive a deceased spouse to take the marital deduction on estate taxes, even if the surviving spouse is not a U.S. citizen.

What Planning Should be in Place for Special Needs Children?

If a special needs child requires governmental assistance, an inheritance may disqualify them from a critical service. Luckily there are specific types of trust that can be set up for those with special needs allowing them to continue to receive benefits and receive their inheritance. However, setting up a special needs trust is complex and specialized. It is important to work with an experienced estate planning attorney to properly protect special needs loved ones.

What Documents Should I have Ready for My College Age Child or High School Senior

When your child turns 18, you no longer legally have the authority to make their medical and financial decisions. So if your child is 18, living out of state for college and gets in a car crash, you risk the doctors not telling you information over the phone. At a minimum, I recommend you have your child designate medical powers of attorney, durable powers of attorney and advanced healthcare directives once they turn 18.

What type of planning do LGBTQ + Couples Need?

The 2015 U.S. Supreme Court ruling that legalized same-sex marriage created new opportunities for gay and lesbian couples who wed to benefit from estate planning strategies that were once out of reach. Couples who completed plans prior to 2015 should have their estate plan reviewed.

I am pregnant, should I wait until my child is born to do an estate plan?

You can start planning your estate while you are pregnant and include language about your future born child.

**Check out your free companion
course for added support and bonuses:**
LegallyEverAfter.com/Resources

GLOSSARY

A

A-B trust planning—A common arrangement used in a will when a married testator has an estate with a value that exceeds his or her remaining estate tax exemption amount. A testator creates at the first death a marital trust or "A Trust" for the sole benefit of the surviving spouse for life (sometimes called a "Marital Trust" or "QTIP Trust") and a bypass or "B Trust" for the benefit of the testator's descendants or the testator's surviving spouse and descendants for life (sometimes called the "Credit Shelter Trust" or "Family Trust"). After the death of the surviving spouse, the remaining assets of both trusts generally pass to the testator's descendants. The B Trust passes at the death of the surviving spouse to the beneficiaries free of estate taxes regardless of the value of the B Trust at that time. The value of the A trust is included in the surviving spouse's estate for estate tax purposes, and the surviving spouse's remaining estate tax exemption is applied to the collective value of the A Trust and the surviving spouse's own assets. Under prior law, only the decedent could use his or her estate tax exemption, so it was important to create the B Trust in order to earmark this exemption.

Administration—The process during which the executor or personal representative collects the decedent's assets, pays all debts and claims, and distributes the residue of the estate according to the will or the state law intestacy rules (when there is no will).

Administrator—The individual or corporate fiduciary appointed by the court to manage an estate if no executor or personal representative has been appointed or if the named executor or personal representative is unable or unwilling to serve.

Annual exclusion—The amount an individual may give annually to each of an unlimited number of recipients free of federal gift or other transfer taxes and with no IRS reporting requirements. In addition, these gifts do not use any of an individual's federal gift tax exemption amount. Payments made directly to providers of education or medical care services also are tax free and do not count against the annual exclusion or gift tax exemption amounts.

Applicable exclusion amount—Another name for the estate tax exemption amount (formerly called the unified credit), which shelters a certain value of assets from the federal estate and gift tax. This amount and inflation are adjusted annually.

Attorney-in-Fact—The person named as agent under a power of attorney to handle the financial affairs of another.

B

Beneficiary—A person who will receive the benefit of property from an estate or trust through the right to receive a bequest or to receive income or trust principal over a period of time.

Bypass trust—The "B Trust" in A-B trust planning that is sheltered from the federal estate tax by the decedent's estate tax exemption amount. Because this trust "bypasses" the estate tax in the decedent's estate and at the surviving spouse's death, this trust often is called a bypass trust. See the comments above concerning A-B trust planning.

C

Charitable lead trust—A trust created during a lifetime or at death that distributes an annuity or unitrust amount to a named charity for life or a term of years, with any remaining trust assets passing to designated non-charitable beneficiaries upon termination of the trust.

Charitable remainder trust—A tax-exempt trust created during a lifetime or at death that distributes an annuity or unitrust amount to one or more designated non-charitable beneficiaries for life or a term of years, with the remaining trust assets passing to charity upon termination of the trust. If appreciated assets are transferred to a charitable remainder trust and sold by the trust, the trust does not pay capital gains tax. Instead, the non-charitable beneficiaries are taxed on a portion of the capital gains as they receive their annual distributions and, in this manner, the capital gains tax is deferred.

Codicil—A formally executed document that amends the terms of a will so that a complete rewriting of the will is not necessary.

Community property—A form of ownership in certain states, known as community property states, under which property acquired during a marriage is presumed to be owned jointly. Only a small number of states are community property states, and the rules can differ significantly in these states.

Conservator—An individual or a corporate fiduciary appointed by a court to care for and manage the property of an incapacitated person, in the same way as a guardian cares for and manages the property of a minor.

Credit shelter trust—Another name for the bypass or "B Trust" in A-B trust planning.

Credit shelter amount—See also *applicable exclusion amount, estate tax exemption amount,* and *unified credit amount.*

Crummey trust—An irrevocable trust that grants a beneficiary of the trust the power to withdraw all or a portion of assets contributed to the trust for a period of time after the contribution. The typical purpose of a Crummey trust is to enable the contributions to the trust to qualify for the annual exclusion from gift tax.

D

Decedent—An individual who has died.

Descendants—An individual's children, grandchildren, and more remote persons who are related by blood or because of legal adoption. An individual's spouse, stepchildren, parents, grandparents, brothers, or sisters are not included. The term "descendants" and "issue" have the same meaning.

Disclaimer—The renunciation or refusal to accept a gift or bequest or the receipt of insurance proceeds, retirement benefits, and the like under a beneficiary designation in order to allow the property to pass to alternate takers. To be a qualified disclaimer and thereby not treated as a gift by the disclaimant (the person who makes the disclaimer), the disclaimer must be made within nine months and before the disclaimant has accepted any interest in the property in order to avoid a tax triggering event. State laws addressing disclaimer may differ, and some wills and trusts might include express provisions governing what happens to assets or interests that are disclaimed. Be certain to consider all these issues before disclaiming.

Durable power of attorney—A power of attorney that does not terminate upon the incapacity of the person making the power of attorney.

E

Estate planning—A process by which an individual designs a strategy and executes a will, trust agreement, or other documents to provide for the administration of his or her assets upon his or her incapacity or death. Tax and liquidity planning are part of this process.

Estate tax—A tax imposed on a decedent's transfer of property at death. An estate tax is to be contrasted with an inheritance tax imposed by certain states on a beneficiary's receipt of property. More than 20 states have state estate taxes that differ from the federal system, so your estate could be subject to a state estate tax even if it is not subject to a federal estate tax.

Estate tax exemption amount—See also *applicable exclusion amount, credit shelter amount,* and *unified credit amount.*

Executor—A person named in a will and appointed by the court to carry out the terms of the will and to administer the decedent's estate. May also be called a personal representative. If a female, may be referred to as the executrix.

F

Family office—An arrangement to coordinate the legal, tax, and other needs of one or more families, either through a true office staffed with employees or through outsourcing to the family's regular advisors. Frequently, a family's private trust company serves as the family office.

Family trust—A trust established to benefit an individual's spouse, children or other family members. A family trust is often the bypass trust or credit shelter trust. *See also A-B trust planning.*

Fiduciary—An individual or a bank or trust company designated to manage money or property for beneficiaries and required to exercise the standard of care set forth in the governing document under which the fiduciary acts and state law. Fiduciaries include executors and trustees.

G

Generation-skipping transfer (GST) tax—A federal tax imposed on outright gifts and transfers in trust, whether during lifetime or at death, to or for beneficiaries two or more generations younger than the donor, such as grandchildren, that exceed the GST tax exemption. The GST tax imposes a tax on transfers that otherwise would avoid gift or estate tax at the skipped generational level. Some states impose a state generation-skipping transfer tax.

Gift tax—The tax on completed lifetime transfers from one individual to or for the benefit of another (other than annual exclusion gifts and certain direct payments to providers of education and medical care) that exceed the gift tax exemption amount. Only the State of Connecticut imposes a separate state gift tax.

Grantor—A person, including a testator, who creates, or contributes property to, a trust. If more than one person creates or contributes property to a trust, each person is a grantor with respect to the portion of the trust property attributable to that person's contribution, except to the extent another person has the power to revoke or withdraw that portion. The grantor is also sometimes referred to as the "settlor," the "trustor," or the "donor." Contrast with the use of the term *grantor trust* to imply a trust the income of which is taxed to the person considered the "grantor" for income tax purposes.

Grantor trust—A trust over which the grantor retains certain control such that the trust is disregarded for federal (and frequently state) income tax purposes, and the grantor is taxed individually on the trust's income and pays the income taxes that otherwise would be payable by the trust or its beneficiaries. Such tax payments are not treated as gifts by the grantor to the trust or its beneficiaries. Provided the grantor does not retain certain powers or benefits, such as a life estate in the trust or the power to revoke the trust, the trust will not be included in the grantor's estate for federal estate tax purposes. Contrast with the non-tax reference to a person who forms or makes gifts to a trust as the "grantor."

Gross estate—A federal estate tax concept that includes all property owned by an individual at death and certain property previously transferred by him or her that is subject to federal estate tax.

GST exemption—The federal tax exclusion that allows a certain value of generation-skipping transfers to be made without the imposition of a generation-skipping tax.

Guardian—An individual or bank or trust company appointed by a court to act for a minor or incapacitated person (the "ward"). A guardian of the person is empowered to make personal decisions for the ward. A guardian of the property (also called a "committee") manages the property of the ward.

H

Health care power of attorney—A document that appoints an individual (an "agent") to make health care decisions when the grantor of the power is incapacitated. Also referred to as a "health care proxy."

Heir—An individual entitled to a distribution of an asset or property interest under applicable state law in the absence of a will. "Heir" and "beneficiary" are not synonymous, although they may refer to the same individual in a particular case.

I

Income—The earnings from principal, such as interest, rent, and cash dividends. This is a fiduciary trust accounting concept and is not the same as taxable income for income tax purposes.

Insurance trust—An irrevocable trust created to own life insurance on an individual or couple and designed to exclude the proceeds of the policy from the insured's gross estate at death.

Interest of a beneficiary—The right to receive income or principal provided in the terms of a trust or will.

Intestate—When one dies without a valid will, such that the decedent's estate is distributed in accordance with a state's intestacy law.

Inventory—A list of the assets of a decedent or trust that is filed with the court.

Irrevocable trust—A trust the grantor cannot terminate or revoke, or otherwise be modified or amended. As modern trust law continues to evolve, however, it may be possible to effect changes to irrevocable trusts through court actions or a process called decanting, which allows the assets of an existing irrevocable trust to be transferred to a new trust with different provisions.

J

Joint tenancy—An ownership arrangement in which two or more persons own property, usually with rights of survivorship.

L

Life beneficiary—An individual who receives income or principal from a trust or similar arrangement for the duration of his or her lifetime.

Life estate—The interest in property owned by a life beneficiary (also called life tenant) with the legal right under state law to use the property for his or her lifetime, after which title fully vests in the remainderman (the person named in the deed, trust agreement, or other legal document as being the ultimate owner when the life estate ends).

Living trust—A trust created by an individual during his or her lifetime, typically as a revocable trust. Also referred to as an "inter vivos" trust. See also r*evocable living trust.*

M

Marital deduction—An unlimited federal estate and gift tax deduction for property passing to a spouse in a qualified manner. In other words, property transfers between spouses generally are not taxable transfers because of the marital deduction.

Marital trust—A trust established to hold property for a surviving spouse in A-B trust planning and designed to qualify for the marital deduction. A commonly used marital trust is a qualified terminable interest property trust. See also *QTIP trust,* which requires that all income must be paid to the surviving spouse.

N

Non-Resident Alien—An individual who is neither a resident nor a citizen of the United States. A non-resident alien nonetheless may be subject to federal estate tax or probate with regard to certain assets situses in the United States. An estate tax treaty between that individual's home country and the United States may affect this result.

No-Contest Clause—A provision in a will or trust agreement that provides that someone who sues to receive more from the estate or trust or overturn the governing document will lose any inheritance rights he or she has. These clauses are not permissible in all instances or in all states.

O

Operation of Law—The way some assets will pass at your death, based on state law or the titling (ownership) of the asset, rather than under the terms of your will.

P

Personal representative—An executor or administrator of a decedent's estate.

Per stirpes—A Latin phrase meaning "per branch" and is a method for distributing property according to the family tree whereby descendants take the share their deceased ancestor would have taken if the ancestor were living. Each branch of the named person's family is to receive an equal share of the estate. If all children are living, each child would receive a share, but if a child is not living, that child's share would be divided equally among the deceased child's children.

Pour over will—A will used in conjunction with a revocable trust to pass title at death to property not transferred to the trust during a lifetime.

Power of appointment—A power given to an individual (usually a beneficiary) under the terms of a trust to appoint property to certain persons upon termination of that individual's interest in the trust or other specified circumstances. The individual given the power is usually referred to as a "holder" of the power. The power of appointment may be general, allowing the property to be appointed to anyone, including the holder, or limited, allowing the property to be distributed to a specified group or to anyone other than the holder. Property subject to a general power of appointment is includible in the holder's gross estate for federal estate tax purposes.

Power of attorney (POA)—Authorization, by a written document, that one individual may act in another's place as agent or attorney-in-fact with respect to some or all legal and financial matters. The scope of authority granted is specified in the document and may be limited by statute in some states. A power of attorney terminates on the death of the person granting the power (unless "coupled with an interest") and may terminate on the subsequent disability of the person granting the power (unless the power is "durable" under the instrument or state law).

Power of withdrawal—A presently exercisable power in favor of the power holder other than a power exercisable in a fiduciary capacity limited by an ascertainable standard, or which is exercisable by another person only upon consent of the trustee or a person holding an adverse interest in the trust.

Principal—The property (such as money, stock, and real estate) contributed to or otherwise acquired by a trust to generate income and to be used for the benefit of trust beneficiaries according to the trust's terms. Also referred to as trust corpus.

Private trust company—An entity formed by a family to serve as fiduciary for the estates and trusts of extended family members. Often referred to as a family trust company.

Probate—The court supervised process of proving the validity of a will and distributing property under the terms of the will or in accordance with a state's intestacy law in the absence of a will.

Probate tax—A tax imposed by many jurisdictions on property passing under an individual's will or by a state's intestacy law.

Property—Anything that may be the subject of ownership, whether real or personal, legal or equitable, or any interest therein.

Prudent man rule—A legal principle requiring a trustee to manage the trust property with the same care that a prudent, honest, intelligent, and diligent person would use to handle the property under the same circumstances. See also *Prudent Investor Act.*

Prudent Investor Act—A law that provides for how fiduciaries must invest trust, estate and other assets they hold in a fiduciary capacity, such as a trustee or executor.

Q

QTIP trust—*See A-B trust planning.*

Qualified domestic trust (QDOT)—A marital trust created for the benefit of a non-U.S. citizen spouse containing special provisions specified by the Internal Revenue Code to qualify for the marital deduction.

Qualified personal residence trust (QPRT)—An irrevocable trust designed to hold title to an individual's residence for a term of years subject to the retained right of the individual to reside in the home for the term, with title passing to children or other beneficiaries at the end of the term.

Qualified terminable interest property (QTIP)—Property held in a marital trust or life estate arrangement that qualifies for the marital deduction because the surviving spouse is the sole beneficiary for life and entitled to all income.

R

Remainder interest—An interest in property owned by the remainderman that does not become possessory until the expiration of an intervening income interest, life estate or term of years.

Residue—The property remaining in a decedent's estate after payment of the estate's debts, taxes, and expenses and after all specific gifts of property and sums of money have been distributed as directed by the will. Also called the residuary estate.

Revocable trust—A trust created during a lifetime over which the grantor reserves the right to terminate, revoke, modify, or amend.

S

S corporation—A corporation that has made a Subchapter S election to be taxed as a pass-through entity (much like a partnership). Certain trusts are permitted to be shareholders only if they make the appropriate elections.

Self-dealing—Personally benefiting from a financial transaction carried out on behalf of a trust or other entity, for example, the purchasing of an asset from a trust by the trustee unless specifically authorized by the trust instrument.

Settlor—Term frequently used for one who establishes or settles a trust. Also called a "trustor" or "grantor."

Special needs trust—Trust established for the benefit of a disabled individual that is designed to allow him or her to be eligible for government financial aid by limiting the use of trust assets for purposes other than the beneficiary's basic care.

Spendthrift provision—A trust provision restricting both voluntary and involuntary transfers of a beneficiary's interest, frequently in order to protect assets from claims of the beneficiary's creditors.

T

Tangible personal property—Property that is capable of being touched and moved, such as personal effects, furniture, jewelry, and automobiles. Tangible personal property is distinguished from intangible personal property that has no physical substance but represents something of value, such as cash, stock certificates, bonds, and insurance policies. Tangible personal property also is distinguished from real property, such as land and items permanently affixed to land, such as buildings.

Tenancy by the entirety—A joint ownership arrangement between a husband and wife, generally with respect to real property, under which the entire property passes to the survivor at the first death and while both are alive, may not be sold without the approval of both.

Tenancy in common—A co-ownership arrangement under which each owner possesses rights and ownership of an undivided interest in the property, which may be sold or transferred by gift during lifetime or at death.

Terms of a trust—The manifestation of the grantor's intent as expressed in the trust instrument or as may be established by other evidence that would be admissible in a judicial proceeding.

Testamentary—Relating to a will or other document effective at death.

Testamentary trust—A trust established in a person's will to come into operation after the will has been probated and the assets have been distributed to it in accordance with the terms of the will.

Testator—A person who signs a will. If a female, may be referred to as the testatrix.

Transfer on death designation—A beneficiary designation for a financial account (and in some states, for real estate) that automatically passes title to the assets at death to a named individual or revocable trust without probate. Frequently referred to as a TOD (transfer on death) or POD (payable on death) designation.

Trust—An arrangement whereby property is legally owned and managed by an individual or corporate fiduciary as trustee for the benefit of another, called a beneficiary, who is the equitable owner of the property.

Trust instrument—A document, including amendments thereto, executed by a grantor that contains terms under which the trust property must be managed and distributed. Also referred to as a trust agreement or declaration of trust.

Trustee—The individual or bank or trust company designated to hold and administer trust property (also generally referred to as a "fiduciary"). The term usually includes original (initial), additional, and successor trustees. A trustee has the duty to act in the best interests of the trust and its beneficiaries and in accordance with the terms of the trust instrument. A trustee must act personally (unless delegation is expressly permitted in the trust instrument), with the exception of certain administrative functions.

U

Unified credit—A credit against the federal gift and estate tax otherwise payable by an individual or estate. Frequently referred to as the estate tax exemption amount, the exemption equivalent, or applicable exclusion amount.

Uniform custodial trust act—A law enacted by some states providing a simple way to create a trust for a minor or adult beneficiary without the need for a complex trust document. Such a trust typically is used for a trust of modest size, particularly for a disabled beneficiary. An adult beneficiary may terminate the trust at any time, otherwise the trust may continue for the life of the beneficiary.

Uniform transfers to minors act—A law enacted by some states providing a convenient means to transfer property to a minor. An adult person known as a "custodian" is designated by the donor to receive and manage property for the benefit of a minor. Although the legal age of majority in many states may be 18, the donor may authorize the custodian to hold the property until the beneficiary reaches age 21. Formerly called the Uniform Gifts to Minors Act.

V

Virtual Representation—A mechanism provided in a will or trust, or in some instances by state law, to permit a beneficiary to make decisions on behalf of another beneficiary who can claim or receive property only under or after them.

W

Will—A document specifying the beneficiaries who are to inherit the testator's assets and naming a representative to administer the estate and be responsible for distributing the assets to the beneficiaries.

APPENDIX I: LEGACY

YOUR LIFE EVENT CHECKLIST

Have any of these events happened to you this year?

If you check one or more boxes below, it's time to create or update your estate plan.

- ☐ You reviewed your estate plan 5 or more years ago
- ☐ Birth of first child, or children have turned 18 (or older)
- ☐ Got married
- ☐ Got divorced or remarried
- ☐ Individuals previously named are no longer appropriate
- ☐ Moved to a different state/relocated to or from a different state
- ☐ Have had a significant increase/decrease in the value of your assets
- ☐ Bought a vacation home or rental property
- ☐ Changed your primary residence
- ☐ You have an IRA, 401(k), or other qualified plan that requires you to begin to take distributions.

APPENDIX II: NAME LEGAL GUARDIANS

LEGAL GUARDIAN CRITERIA

Five easy steps to naming legal guardians to protect your children:

- Step One: Each partner brainstorms a list of potential guardian names separately.
- Step Two: Create a list of your values.
- Step Three: Rank each person or couple based on the criteria below.

Criteria	Relationship with Kids	Similar Parenting Style	Location	Total
Steve & Mary	10	4	6	20
Greg & Danielle	7	7	2	16
Sara	5	3	3	11
Nicole & Patrick	9	1	4	14

Criteria	Relationship with Kids	Similar Parenting Style	Location	Total
Couple 1				
Couple 2				
Individual 1				
Individual 2				

- Step Four: combine your lists with your partner's list and select the top three together.
- Step Five: Finalize the guardian nominations in a legal document.

APPENDIX III: ECONOMIC SUPPORT

THE DIFFERENCE BETWEEN A WILL AND TRUST

	Living Trust	Will
Avoids Probate Costs	☑ Yes	No
Provide for your care during a disability	☑ Yes	No
Quickly Settled	☑ Yes	No
Leave property to minor children	☑ Yes	No
Keep privacy after death	☑ Yes	No
Protection from court challenges	☑ Yes	No
Asset Protection	☑ Yes	No
Minimize Estate Taxes	☑ Yes	No

APPENDIX IV: EXPRESSING WISHES

CREATE AN INSTRUCTIONS TO GUARDIANS MEMORANDUM

An Instructions to Guardians Memorandum provides guidance to the guardians of your minor children if you are unable to care for your children due to death or disability. The memorandum gives guidance with respect to those decisions you consider most important when raising your children, including education, religion and discipline, children-rearing practices, financial considerations, and your wishes regarding your children's care.

The memorandum can be in written form, or you can record your answers to the following questions. Whichever form you decide to create, the important thing is that you communicate your wishes to the guardians before something happens to you or inform them of where they can find this documentation if something were to happen to you.

The following items can be included in this memorandum:

1. **List of Important Family Members and Friends.** This list provides the names of friends and family members that are extremely important to you and your request that

every effort should be made for these people to maintain a relationship with our children.

2. **Medical Information.** You should list out the current treatment providers for your children, any allergies, conditions, treatments and prescriptions.

3. **Activities and Extracurriculars.** You should list out which extracurricular programs and activities that are important to your children.

   a. Include lessons and clubs that they are interested in, or plan to join at a later date.

   b. Also include any activities that you have decided as a family that they *shouldn't* do.

4. **Financial.** While you have structured in your estate plan to provide for your children financially through your living trust you may have additional financial guidance include the following:

   a. We consider the following priorities the most important when it comes to the use of the financial resources we have left for our children:

   b. We would like our children to receive an allowance at the following ages and in the following amounts:

   c. We would like our guardian to teach our children the value of money in the following ways:

   d. The following is a list of items we would expect our children to ask us for money and which we would help him or her with, if asked:

5. **Community**

   a. We would like our children to be introduced to the following organizations and activities that support the community:

   b. We have the following charitable inclinations and would like these to be further developed in our children:

6. **Values**
   a. The personal values that are most important to us and that we would like our children to have a strong understanding about are as follows:

7. **Religion and Spirituality**
   a. Our children have been raised in the following religion or tradition:
   b. It is important to us that our children observe the following holidays:
   c. It is important to us that our children participate in the following religious community:

8. **Education**
   a. We strongly prefer that our children attend: (select as appropriate) public, private, home, other type of schooling (describe).
   b. In selecting and monitoring our children's educational experiences, it is important to us that the guardian be closely involved in our children's education by:
   c. In addition, it is important that our guardian round out our children's education by providing opportunities outside of the classroom to enjoy:

9. **Discipline**
   a. The following methods of discipline are totally unacceptable to us, and if our guardian feels he or she requires these methods, we wish that person to decline to accept guardianship of our children:
   b. The following methods of discipline are those we use most frequently because we believe they are appropriate and effective:

10. **Parenting Resources**
    a. The following resources (books, organizations, etc.) have been helpful to us as we have developed our parenting philosophy. We encourage our children's guardian to consider these resources for himself or herself:

You can view an example Instructions to Guardian Memorandum on LegallyEverAfter.com/resources.

FINANCIAL AND EDUCATION LITERACY

Financial literacy and education with your children should include both general financial topics that everyone needs to know (i.e., creating a budget, savings and balancing a checkbook) and financial topics specific to your wealth (i.e., real estate investing and stock investing).

The following are financial education topics based on your child's age:

Pre-schoolers, First and Second Grade

1. Earning Money through allowance. Children learn that money isn't free. Children do certain tasks around the home as a family member. Children are also given the opportunity to do additional bonus tasks and earn an allowance.
2. Spending plans and goal setting. Teach your children they can create goals for their money through a spending plan. They can either save the money, spend it, or share it. When they get older, expand to other options—including investing.

Grades 3- 6

1. Money and Responsibility - responsible money management starts with keeping records of what is spent and what is saved. Teach your children how to track their purchases and savings.
2. Investing - teach your kids about interest rates and investing in stocks. Purchase a stock from a company your child knows and have them track it over a time period.

3. Needs versus Wants - help your child understand the difference between needs and wants. Walk around the house and have your child categorize things as needs versus wants.

4. Sharing - teach your child about sharing through donating to causes and charities or doing fundraising activities. Have them choose a charity and follow how the funds help people.

Teens

1. Budgeting - help your teen understand how much money they need for a car, car insurance, gas and other expenses. Teach them about budgeting and cashflow.

2. Investing - help older children understand more advanced investing topics like market volatility and asset diversification. Set up a custodial brokerage account and teach them how to invest.

3. Family Business - if you have a family business, get them involved with different parts of the business.

Early adulthood:

1. Investments - parents should give their children more advanced education around investments and retirement planning.

2. Other topics specific to your family. Parents should involve children in annual meetings with financial advisor, CPA and attorneys.

ABOUT THE AUTHOR

Pamela Maass Garrett is an Estate Planning Attorney, mother, wife, entrepreneur and CEO of Law Mother LLC, a law firm she founded to help parents protect their futures and loved ones. Planted in Colorado, Pamela focuses her practice on helping families and business owners protect their future and loved ones. Pamela started her career as a Deputy District Attorney, she has over 40 jury trials under her belt, and she uses her litigation experience to help her clients plan in a way to keep their loved ones out of court and conflict. Prior to law school, Pamela earned her B.S. in Industrial Engineering, M.S. in Civil Engineering and enjoys using innovative technology to improve her clients' experiences with legal planning.

Made in United States
North Haven, CT
27 October 2023